LOVE Is PATIENT, but I'M NOT

LOVE Is PATIENT, but I'M NOT

Confessions of a
Recovering Perfectionist

CHRISTOPHER WEST

BEACON PUBLISHING
North Palm Beach, Florida

Unless otherwise noted, Scripture passages have been taken from the *Revised
Standard Version, Catholic Edition*. Copyright © 1946, 1952, 1971 by the Division of
Christian Education of the National Council of Churches of Christ in the USA. Used
by permission. All rights reserved.

Scripture texts marked NAB in this work are taken from the *New American Bible*,
revised edition © 2010, 1991, 1986, 1970 Confraternity of Christian Doctrine,
Washington, D.C. and are used by permission of the copyright owner. All rights
reserved. No part of the *New American Bible* may be reproduced in any form without
permission in writing from the copyright owner.

Quotes are taken from the English translation of the *Catechism of the Catholic Church*
for the United States of America (indicated as *CCC*), 2nd edition. Copyright © 1997
by United States Catholic Conference—Libreria Editrice Vaticana.

Quoted material from Pope Francis is taken from *The Joy of Love*, published by
Beacon Publishing, 2015.

Design by Madeline Harris
Interior by Ashley Wirfel

ISBN: 978-1-63582-006-5 (softcover)
ISBN: 978-1-929266-66-1 (e-book)

Library of Congress Cataloging-in-Publication Data
Names: West, Christopher, 1969- author.
Title: Love is patient, but I'm not : confessions of a recovering
perfectionist / Christopher West.
Description: North Palm Beach, Florida : Beacon Publishing, Inc., 2017.
Identifiers: LCCN 2017034043 | ISBN 9781635820065 (softcover) | ISBN
9781929266661 (e-book)
Subjects: LCSH: Bible. Corinthians, 1st, XIII, 4-7—Criticism,
interpretation, etc. | Love—Biblical teaching. | Love—Religious
aspects—Catholic Church.
Classification: LCC BS2675.52 .W47 2017 | DDC
241/.4—dc23

Dynamic Catholic® and Be Bold. Be Catholic.® and The Best Version of Yourself®
are registered trademarks of The Dynamic Catholic Institute.

For more information on this title or other books and CDs available through the
Dynamic Catholic Book Program,
please visit www.DynamicCatholic.com.

The Dynamic Catholic Institute
5081 Olympic Blvd • Erlanger • Kentucky • 41018
Phone: 1–859–980–7900
Email: info@DynamicCatholic.com

Second printing, January 2018

Printed in the United States of America

Other Books by
CHRISTOPHER WEST

Good News about Sex & Marriage:
Answers to Your Honest Questions about Catholic Teaching

Theology of the Body Explained:
A Commentary on John Paul II's Man and Woman He Created Them

Theology of the Body for Beginners:
Rediscovering the Meaning of Life, Love, Sex, and Gender

The Love That Satisfies:
Reflections on Eros and Agape

Heaven's Song:
Sexual Love as It Was Meant to Be

At the Heart of the Gospel:
Reclaiming the Body for the New Evangelization

Fill These Hearts:
God, Sex, and the Universal Longing

Pope Francis to Go:
Bite-Sized Morsels from The Joy of the Gospel

Theology of the Body at the Movies

CONTENTS

INTRODUCTION

I grew up believing that I was only "lovable" if I got my act together. I had to be a "good boy" to be worthy of God's love, or anyone else's. Be perfect (read: be a "saint") and then you'll be loved. Such was the impression made on me by a falsely pious upbringing.

Having shared my story with audiences around the world, I know I'm not the only recovering perfectionist out there. It's a sadly common but tragically misguided impression of what it means to be Catholic. There is so much wrong with this view, not the least of which is what it means to be a saint. Saints are not perfect people. They are people who know that they are perfectly loved in all their imperfections. They *abide* in that love and it fills them with the infectious joy of the gospel. "Abide in my love," says Jesus, "that my joy may be in you, and that your joy may be full" (John 15:9, 11).

The irresistible promise of joy, of satisfying our heart's hunger for love—isn't that what we're all looking for? Isn't that why we do crazy things . . . like get married?

Wendy and I were all about that joy when we tied the knot. In fact, along with our wedding date, 11/18/95, we'd had the jeweler inscribe a personal adaptation of Christ's promise on the underside of our rings. Although scratched and worn, they're still legible today: Mine reads *your joy in us* and hers reads *our joy complete.*

Like all young couples, Wendy and I had a rather naive understanding of what the joy of love entailed when we ventured into married life. Joy, Pope Francis explains, refers to "an expansion of the heart" and it "needs to be cultivated." Paradoxically, that happens amid sorrow. Cultivating true joy "involves accepting that marriage is an inevitable mixture of enjoyment and struggles, tensions and repose, pain and relief, satisfactions and longings, annoyances and pleasures, but always on the path of friendship, which inspires married couples to care for one another" (*The Joy of Love,* 126). As countless couples can attest, it's that care for one another over the long haul that slowly births the deep, abiding joy of love.

Having been disillusioned and deeply wounded by the secular culture's approach to love and sexuality, I spent my early twenties immersing myself in Catholic teaching on man and woman, especially Pope John Paul II's Theology of the Body. As a newlywed, I was completing my graduate work at the Pontifical Institute for Studies on Marriage and Family. I had plenty of book knowledge about the divine plan for human love, but the journey from head to heart would be a long and rocky one. Right around our first anniversary, someone asked us how married life had been going. I smiled at Wendy and boasted, "You know, a lot of people say the first year of marriage can be really difficult, but it's been easy for us." Years later my wife would tell me, "That's when I knew you were utterly clueless."

Mercy. . . . That cluelessness was to last another nine years or so.

It wasn't that I was oblivious to various tensions. We had our ups and downs, like any couple. But overall the first ten years of married life seemed great to me. I had a wonderful wife and awesome kids; I was getting lots of accolades traveling the world as a best-selling author and lecturer; and during our tenth year of marriage, I was offered a lucrative book deal by the biggest publishing house in the world. My ship had come in. Or so it seemed. Little did I know my ship was taking on water, and some major storms were just on the horizon. As I would come to learn through various painful trials, I was wearing a lot of masks. And I was looking to my marriage to fill an infinite hunger for love that only the Infinite One can fill.

"Each marriage is a kind of 'salvation history,'" observes Pope Francis, "which from fragile beginnings—thanks to God's gift and a creative and generous response on our part—grows over time into something precious and enduring" (*The Joy of Love*, 221). The reflections I offer here provide a glimpse into various chapters of that ongoing salvation history. I share some rather personal stories from my own marriage and throughout my life—not to draw attention to myself, but in hopes of inspiring readers to take a closer look at their own lives and relationships and, in doing so, open more deeply to God's mercy.

Someone who read an advance copy of the manuscript said he thought a few of my reflections could be summed up as follows: "My life is a mess and my wife is a saint." It's certainly true that I'm more candid in sharing my own faults. I'm not at liberty to expose someone else's (where I do, I have my wife's permission).

The idea for this book came from a priest friend. He and I had been sharing how much we both appreciated what Pope Francis has called "the heart" of his document *The Joy of Love*: his penetrating meditations on St. Paul's famous hymn to love in 1 Corinthians 13. "That section of the document would make a great examination of conscience," he said in passing. Guess what he gave me as a penance after my confession.

As you'll see, each short chapter is based on one line of St. Paul's magnificent hymn to love. The quotations in bold come straight from Pope Francis' document *The Joy of Love*. My personal stories and considerations follow to illuminate his points. The reflection questions at the end of each section are intended to help you open perhaps previously unexposed places in your own life's story to God's healing light. Journaling is an excellent way to "pour out your heart" before the Lord (see Psalm 62), so consider getting yourself a notebook you can use to write down your thoughts.

While many of the lessons I've learned flow from my experience as a married man, these reflections are not only intended for married people. Regardless of a person's state in life, every one of us is involved in a great variety of human relationships, all of which can benefit from entering more deeply into St. Paul's hymn to love.

The one goal in all of this is for you, the reader, to come away with a deeper, richer experience of God's unconditional and infinitely merciful love *for you*. Only to the degree that we have received this love are we able to share it with others. Indeed, everything that Pope Francis teaches about showing love to others, as he himself says, "assumes that we ourselves have ... known a love that is prior to any of our own efforts.... If we accept that God's love is unconditional . . . then we will become capable of showing boundless love [to others]" (*Joy of Love*, 108).

This, I believe, takes us to the very heart of who Pope Francis is, what he believes, and what he is tirelessly trying to teach the Church and the world: God's unconditional love is the foundation of absolutely *everything* the Church is and, hence, is the fundamental gift the Church has to share with the world. If we are defenders of the Church's teaching, proclaiming all her doctrines from the rooftops, but have not love, we are a resounding gong or a clashing cymbal. And if we comprehend all God's mysteries, know all there is to know in this world, and have faith to move mountains, but have not love, we are nothing. And if we give away everything we own and hand over our very lives to be sacrificed, but have not love, we gain nothing.

Love is patient and kind;
love is not jealous or boastful;
it is not arrogant or rude.
Love does not insist on its own way,
it is not irritable or resentful;
it does not rejoice at wrong,
but rejoices in the right.
Love bears all things,
believes all things,
hopes all things,
endures all things.
(1 Corinthians 13:4–7)

ONE

Love Is Patient

[The meaning of patience] is clarified by the Greek translation of the Old Testament, where we read that God is "slow to anger" (Ex 34:6; Num 14:18). It refers, then, to the quality of one who does not act on impulse and avoids giving offense. (91)

Kids' messes. They try my patience.

I'm a preventive maintenance kind of guy with a penchant for spotting potential messes before they happen. My kids are quite familiar with paternal refrains like: "Keep your bowl away from the edge of the table" (to avoid a spill); "Make sure all the pasta is poured into the strainer" (so I don't have to labor to clean calcified noodles off the pot later on); "Be sure to wipe Mandy's paws when she comes in the house" (so I don't have to clean the carpet).

I can be a bit obsessive, and it gets under my kids' skin—understandably. They can be rather careless, and that gets under my skin—understandably. But if love is patient, what does love do in such a situation? As Pope Francis rightly insists, it "does not immediately react harshly to the weaknesses and faults of others" (*The Joy of Love,* 103).

Recently I walked into our family room and spotted a new deck of cards on the coffee table with no rubber band around them. I foresaw the inevitable—cards strewn everywhere and *yet another* deck of cards rendered useless because we couldn't find them all—and my immediate internal reaction was: *What the #*$%@!!...Who the #*$%@!!* My external reaction may have been more measured, but the stress in my voice barely masked what was going on inside when I barked: *"Who knows anything about these cards?"*

"They're just cards," quipped Beth, asserting her and her siblings' right to live in our house and play cards without fearing their father's neatnik need for control. She wasn't being disrespectful; she was just stating (rightly) that it's not the big deal I was making it out to be. Not wanting to admit that my thirteen-year-old had just called me on the weeds of impatience in my soul, I blurted out, "That's not what I mean, Beth." In other words, "You think I'm in control-freak mode again, but I'm not."

I was. And I knew it. And, clearly, she knew it. In her own frustrated way my daughter was saying, "Love is patient, Dad. And you're not loving your family right now." She was right. It took me a few days of internal wrestling to sort out what had actually happened in that exchange, but when I did, I apologized to Beth for my impatience.

Pope Francis insightfully observes that we "encounter problems whenever we think that relationships or people ought to be perfect, or when we put ourselves at the center and expect things to turn out our way. Then everything makes us impatient, everything makes us react aggressively. Unless we cultivate patience," he concludes, "we will always find excuses for responding angrily" (*The Joy of Love*, 92).

Love is patient. Oftentimes, I am not.
Lord, teach me to love.

How do I respond when others inconvenience me or act in some way that I'd rather they didn't? Am I quick to react with dismay, disdain, or aggression?

What experiences shaped me growing up that may be affecting the way I respond to others' and my own faults throughout the day?

Patience takes root when I recognize that other people also have a right to live in this world, just as they are. It does not matter if they hold me back, if they unsettle my plans, or annoy me by the way they act or think, or if they are not everything I want them to be. Love always has an aspect of deep compassion that leads to accepting the other person as part of this world, even when he or she acts differently than I would like. (92)

Remember the "cool" kids at school or in the neighborhood? I *had* to be one of them. I had to be part of the in crowd growing up. And that, among other things, meant dressing a certain way, acting a certain way, listening to certain music, and ostracizing everyone who was other than we were. The "world of cool" essentially gets divided into two categories: those who *are* and those who *aren't*. It was all a facade, of course, that masked a deep personal insecurity, a deep fear of rejection, a deep fear that behind the masks I wasn't lovable.

Without a thorough interior conversion that reveals the web of lies behind the charade, those patterns of thinking don't just go away with time. I brought them with me from my teens into my twenties and right into my marriage. And it wrought some painful havoc.

Wendy learned at a young age that one's true sense of worth is not to be found in playing the game of being cool. While I hid behind a facade growing up, she was relatively at peace with who she was. I was profoundly attracted to her because of that, and at the same time profoundly threatened by it. The profoundly attracted part compelled me to ask her to marry me, and sadly, the profoundly threatened part compelled me to try to mold her in my image. Early in our relationship I took it upon myself to "help" Wendy learn how to be just as cool as I was. Subtly and sometimes not-so-subtly, I was evaluating her in light of the arbitrary standards I had swallowed growing up.

And here's the sickness of it all: I actually believed it was the loving and caring thing to do to help my wife learn how to think and act more like I did. In reality the message I was sending was: *If you want to be loved and accepted, then you have to hide your true self and wear just as many masks as I'm wearing.* Mercy.

Patience takes root, Pope Francis tells us, when we learn to love people just as they are, not as we want them to be. Patience accepts the other person even when he or she acts differently than I would like. In this sense, I was not always patient with Wendy. It was several years into our marriage before I began to wake up to these patterns of thinking and take an honest look at my many masks and how they prevented me from loving myself and others. All the while my wife was showing me that "aspect of deep compassion" Pope Francis talks about—knowing I was causing her that pain because I myself was in it.

Love embraces people just as they are.
Sometimes I don't. Lord, teach me how to love.

Am I willing to give people room to be who they are—foibles and all—without demanding they be who I want (or need) them to be?

When I'm quick (internally or externally) to criticize people who annoy me because of the way they act or think, what underlying attitudes do I use to justify the idea that these people should think or act the way I do? Is there some hurt or rejection in my own life that I'm attempting to soothe by allowing myself to feel superior to others?

Write a simple prayer of your own, asking for the grace of patience toward yourself and others.

TWO

Love Is Kind

The next word that Paul uses is *chrestéuetai*. The word is used only here in the entire Bible. It is derived from *chrestós*: a good person, one who shows his goodness by his deeds. . . . The word indicates that love benefits and helps others. For this reason it is translated as "kind"; love is ever ready to be of assistance. (93)

It was a late flight after a long day teaching a parish seminar. I was tired. And hungry. A mad rush at the airport meant I hadn't had time for dinner, and no meal was being offered on the flight. All I had to feed my growling stomach was an oversized oatmeal raisin cookie I had stuffed in my bag earlier that day, a leftover from one of those boxed lunches. Not much of a meal, but if I could just get a little cold milk to go with it, it would make it a bit of a treat. Cookies without milk, in my book, aren't worth much.

I knew from years of travel that asking a flight attendant for a cup of milk is a hit-or-miss proposition. They have milk on board for tea and coffee, but it's not typically offered as a beverage.

"What would you like to drink?"

"Could I possibly get a cup of milk?"

"Sorry, we don't serve milk on this flight."

Bummer. I settled for water. And sulked a bit.

Soon thereafter another flight attendant walked by. She must have seen the look of disappointment on my face, because she stopped and bent down to address me at eye level. She was an older woman with a look of genuine concern on her face, almost motherly. "Do you need something?" she asked thoughtfully.

"Well," I started to explain, "I know you aren't serving milk on this—"

Before I could even finish my sentence, having glanced at my cellophane-wrapped cookie next to my cup of water, she properly assessed my craving, and gently placing her hand on my arm, she said, "Let me see what I can do."

Her kindness, her readiness to be of assistance in fulfilling my little personal desire, however trivial it was, caught me off guard. A lump welled up in my throat and my eyes started to water as she went on her mission with no other desire, it seemed, than to bless me. She soon appeared with two little cartons of milk and the kindest of smiles. "There you go!" she said, with a caring twinkle in her eye. And I thought of Christ's words: "And whoever gives to one of these little ones even a cup of cold water [ahem, milk] . . . he will not lose his reward" (Matthew 10:42).

> Sometimes I overlook the needs and desires of others. Love is kind. It is ever ready to be of assistance. Lord, teach me to love.

What's a similar story from my own life when someone blessed me with an unexpected act of kindness? How was God's personal love for me working through that person?

How can I be more attentive to the needs and desires of others in my life? What are some ways I can sacrifice my own needs and desires to help fulfill those of others?

Throughout the text, it is clear that Paul wants to stress that love is more than a mere feeling. Rather, "to love" . . . is "to do good." [Love] shows its fruitfulness and allows us to experience the happiness of giving, the nobility and grandeur of spending ourselves unstintingly, without asking to be repaid, purely for the pleasure of giving and serving. (94)

I had various manual labor jobs in my teens and early twenties, and they were always drudgery to me. I would slog my way through them for one reason: a paycheck.

When my older brother Soren asked me if I could help him build a fence for a neighbor of his, I wasn't exactly jumping at the chance to thicken my calluses, but I knew it was humbling for my brother both to accept this job and to ask for my help. He and his new bride had enthusiastically started a vintage art and framing shop eighteen months earlier. They had a newborn baby and countless unpaid bills; their shop was going under. His financial straits were just the latest in a long line of hard knocks he had endured throughout his life. I was single at the time with few responsibilities, so I agreed to help.

It turned out to be an extremely difficult job. Unfortunately, Soren had offered his neighbor a flat rate for the work (rather than time and materials), and the profits were getting eaten up with every unexpected rock we encountered digging postholes. I could feel a lifetime of frustration welling up in my brother. It finally exploded when, with one heaving thrust, he struck a boulder, broke the posthole digger, and injured his hand. He went into a rage like I'd never seen and stormed off the site, leaving me to face the rocks on my own.

I took a deep breath, looked heavenward for help, and got busy. To my surprise, I labored peacefully by myself until sunset, digging as many rocks out of the ground as I could. Something inside me had shifted; I had received a particular grace. I was not working for a paycheck. I was laboring for love of my brother. And that changed the whole experience. It changed what otherwise would have been a hellish day for me into an experience of "the happiness of giving."

That taste that day of what Pope Francis calls "the nobility and grandeur of spending ourselves . . . purely for the pleasure of giving and serving" has been a lesson I've carried with me ever since: Even drudgery can be transformed into love, and that makes all the difference.

Love gives and serves happily without expecting to be repaid.

Lord, when I'm focused on myself, spending myself for others is a burden I'd prefer to avoid. Teach me to love!

When I'm confronted with my own selfishness in light of the call to sacrifice myself for others, how do I respond? Do I cave in or do I cry out?

Do I act as though I have recourse only to my own frailties in serving others?

St. Teresa of Calcutta would often say that we must love "until it hurts." What is my honest reaction to that idea?

Do I honestly serve others *for others*, expecting nothing in return? Or are my motives mixed with my own desire for the praise of others, to be seen as a virtuous person?

THREE

Love Is Not Jealous

[Not being jealous] means that love has no room for discomfiture at another person's good fortune (cf. Acts 7:9; 17:5). Envy is a form of sadness provoked by another's prosperity; it shows that we are not concerned for the happiness of others but only with our own well-being. (95)

I love old houses—farmhouses, cottages, stone or log homes—especially if they're tucked away in the woods. I'm blessed to live in such a home. It's the kind of place I've dreamed of living in since I was a little kid. And the circumstances surrounding how we acquired it had God's smiling providence all over it.

The house (a log cabin built in the early 1800s with a stone addition) and the property (mostly wooded, with a home office off the garage) have everything I dreamed of—*except* . . . except a creek running through it. I love creeks. The very word conjures up sounds, smells, memories, and mysteries that make my heart sing. Sometimes when I drive by a gorgeous old home tucked back in the woods next to a creek, I find myself wondering how *that* family got so lucky. Rather than resting in gratitude for the beautiful home with which God has blessed me, I can find myself wondering why *I* didn't get a property with a creek.

What kind of rearranging of my soul needs to take place for my first reaction to be, "Wow, what a gorgeous property—I'm so happy for whoever lives there"?

> Love is not jealous. Sometimes I am.
> Lord, teach me to love.
>
> ---
>
> When other people prosper in ways I desire to prosper, am I happy for them or only sad for myself?
>
> Am I grateful for and content with the good things God has blessed me with? Do I sometimes grumble that I haven't been granted what so-and-so has?
>
> Am I generous in sharing my good fortune with others? How can I be more so?

Whereas love makes us rise above ourselves, envy closes us in on ourselves. True love values the other person's achievements. It does not see him or her as a threat. It frees us from the sour taste of envy. It recognizes that everyone has different gifts and a unique path in life. So it strives to discover its own road to happiness, while allowing others to find theirs. (95)

A few years ago I started having dreams about someone I knew in high school named Jeremy. Then memories of how poorly I treated him were coming back to me during my times of prayer. These were clear nudges that there were some things from my past that I needed to revisit both for the sake of my own inner growth and for the sake of righting some old wrongs.

Jeremy was a year behind me in school, and, for reasons I couldn't explain back then, he just bugged me. He was just *different*; as a result, I made a point to single him out for all kinds of taunts and insults. One day he was walking a few paces ahead of me with a loaded book bag draped over his shoulder. I noticed a little tear in the corner and gleefully ripped it wide open, then ran away laughing as he labored to gather his belongings.

Nearly thirty years later I was trying to take an honest look at why I had been so annoyed by Jeremy, why I couldn't just let him be. When I asked God to shine his light on these memories, it didn't take long to find the answer.

Jeremy was one of those kids who just didn't care about what other people thought of him. He wasn't caught up, as I was, in trying to conform to other people's standards and expectations. And I hated him for it. Truth is, I was jealous. He had a freedom about him, a freedom to be himself that deep down I desperately wanted but didn't think I could ever achieve. As an insecure teenage boy, I resented the heck out of the fact that Jeremy wasn't as bound up as I was. His freedom was a constant reminder of my lack thereof. Envy, in turn, manifested itself as cruelty.

With a quick Google search, I found his contact information and sent him the following e-mail:

Dear Jeremy,

    This is Christopher West writing. I'm not even sure if you remember me, but this may jar your memory. I was a year ahead of you at

Catholic High and, to put it frankly, I was a real ass to you. And that, in fact, is why I'm writing.

I know this is totally out of the blue and may seem strange, but I've been doing some soul searching lately in my life and trying to make amends for some of the crap I dished out on people. And you've come to mind several times as someone I need to apologize to. So I typed your name into Google and found your e-mail.

It looks like we're both still in the area. I'm wondering if you'd let me take you out to lunch sometime.

He agreed and we chatted for a couple of hours at a local coffee shop. Turns out he'd had a reversion to his faith since high school, just as I'd had. That made our conversation flow all the more naturally. I was honest with him about how my high school cruelty had masked an inner jealousy. I apologized sincerely and asked him to forgive me. He graciously did. I think we both left that meeting a little lighter.

> ## Lord, I'm sorry that my jealousy has hurt others. Teach me to love.
>
> ---
>
> Who are the people in my life, past or present,
> whom I've felt threatened by because of their achievements?
> Have I harbored resentment toward them?
> Have I been cruel to them because of hidden envy?

Are there relationships in my life, past or present, in need of healing because of the ways I've behaved in my jealousy?

How can I honestly rejoice in the gifts, talents, and achievements of others?

FOUR

Love Is Not Boastful

The . . . word, *perpereúetai* [boastful], denotes vainglory, the need to be haughty, pedantic and somewhat pushy. Those who love not only refrain from speaking too much about themselves, but are focused on others; they do not need to be the center of attention. (97)

I have found that there are four kinds of Catholics: those who love the movie *Nacho Libre*,[1] those who despise it, those who just don't get it, and—the vast majority—those who've never heard of it.

I fall into the first category. It is a rare day in my family when someone has not quoted a line from our extensive library of Nacho-isms. Not only does Jack Black's character, Ignacio—a Franciscan friar who secretly becomes pro wrestler Nacho—make me laugh uproariously, I honestly believe there is some mystical nectar to be savored amid the absolute absurdity of it all.

The most important lesson Ignacio learns comes straight out of the gospel: "If I glorify myself," says Jesus, "my glory is nothing; it is my Father who glorifies me" (John 8:54). Ignacio is tired of

---

[1] All quotes taken from *Nacho Libre*, directed by Jared Hess (Hollywood, Calif.: Paramount Pictures, 2006).

being a nobody among the other friars at the monastery ("The brothers . . . don't think I know a butt load o' crap about the gospel, but I doooooooo."), and he covets from afar the glory of the famous *luchadores* (Mexican wrestlers) who "get all the fancy ladies, and the clothes, and the free creams and lotions." At one point, trying to recruit Steven as his tag team partner, he exclaims, "Don't you wanna little taste o' the glory, see what it tastes like?"

It's clear that Ignacio wants a taste: "I am the gatekeeper of my own destiny, and I will have my glory day in the hot sun."

But Nacho's road to glory is paved with disappointments and humiliations because, well, he's trying to glorify himself. It's all about him. Despite all his desperate attempts to acquire "nutrients" and "eagle powers" so he can prove his prowess in the ring, he keeps losing. He even baptizes Steven with a surprise face dunk before squaring off against Satan's Cavemen in hopes of securing the victory (and because, as he explains, "I'm a little concerned right now, about your salvation and stuff").

Sister Encarnación tries to warn Ignacio: "You are a man of the cloth. . . . These men fight for vanity, for money, for false pride."

Ignacio, always wanting to agree with this lovely nun (his wrestling with his feelings for her is another humorously and insightfully, if sometimes irreverently, handled theme of the movie), responds, "Yes, it's terrible, terrible. But is it always a sin to fight?"

"No," responds the comely nun. "If you fight for something noble, or for someone who needs your help, only then will God bless you in battle."

Ignacio's turning point comes when he prays, kneeling before the altar: "Precious Father, why have you given me this desire to wrestle and then made me such a stinky warrior? Have I focused too much on my boots, and on fame, and on my stretchy pants?" Then, in a moment of astonished illumination, he says to God, "Wait a second... maybe you want me to fight and give everything I win to the little ones who have nothing, so they can have better foods and a better life." At that moment a candle drops to the floor and sets his Franciscan robes aflame, a comedic indication that the Spirit has descended on Ignacio.

With his robes charred away, the other brothers see his "stretchy pants" underneath and he confesses that he is, in fact, "Nachooooooooooooooooooooooo!" the *luchadore.* "Tonight," he says, "I will fight the seven strongest men in town, maybe the world. And I will win because our heavenly Father will be in the ring with me. And he and I will win ten thousand pesos." Then, choking on tears, he announces, "And with it, I will buy the orphans a big bus to go on field trips to parks and places like that." Finally, perusing the incredulous expressions of his brothers, he shouts, *"I'm serious!"*

Before the championship bout, Steven, who up to this point "only believe[d] in *science,*" prays for Nacho: "Dear Lord, please bless Nacho with nutrients and strength," and Nacho says with him, "Amen!" In the final minutes of battle, the long-desired eagle powers descend upon him, and Nacho becomes the new champion. At last he gets "a little taste o' the glory," but this time, he hasn't grasped at it; it's a gift bestowed from above. And, of course, he doesn't keep the glory for himself, but shares it with the orphans. Another lesson from above: "I have given them the glory you gave me" (John 17:22, NAB). Pretty deep lessons for a ridiculous comedy.

Love is not boastful. It does not seek glory or to be the center of attention. Sometimes, like Nacho, I do. Lord, teach me to love.

———————————————

How do I seek to draw attention to myself?
What am I looking for when I do so?

"If I glorify myself," says Jesus, "my glory is nothing; but it is my Father who glorifies me" (John 8:54).
What does this mean in my own life?

Write a simple prayer of your own asking for the grace to trust in the Father's gift of glory and renouncing all desire to glorify yourself.

FIVE

Love Is Not Arrogant

Paul . . . says that "knowledge puffs up," whereas "love builds up" (1 Cor 8:1). Some think that they are important because they are more knowledgeable than others; they want to lord it over them. Yet what really makes us important is a love that understands, shows concern, and embraces the weak. (97)

I remember clearly the astonishing moment I *knew* I would never let this woman go, the moment I knew I had found a treasure beyond imagining in Wendy Weidman, and that if she would have me, I would spend the rest of my life with her.

A mutual friend had introduced us in our college years. We went to different schools, but our campuses were close to each other, and we enjoyed a nice friendship for a few years before anything turned romantic. Wendy was actually the first person ever to invite me to give a talk on the Theology of the Body. I had only recently discovered John Paul II's teaching when she heard me casually sharing some things about it and asked if I would mind addressing her campus ministry group. I took note at the end of my presentation that Wendy was asking some very intelligent questions. It was my first inkling that she and I might have a future together, but it wasn't the moment I *knew*.

After college, Wendy moved to New Jersey to help take care of her grandparents, both of whom were in their eighties. They themselves were also still caring for the surviving matriarch of the family, Wendy's 105-year-old great-grandmother, whom she affectionately called Nana. It was the day I met Nana that I knew I'd never let go of Wendy. Well, I didn't actually *meet* Nana. She was blind and nearly deaf, and wasn't even aware I was in the room. What did happen that day, though, changed the course of my life.

I had come to visit Wendy in New Jersey, and one of the top things on her list was to take me to see Nana, who was now receiving round-the-clock care at a nearby nursing home. Walking through the front doors, I realized I hadn't been in an "old folks' home" since my own great-grandmother had died, in 1976. Walking down the hall past several feeble, wheelchair-bound souls, I noticed immediately that, while I was tightening up and drawing inward with discomfort, Wendy was completely at ease and outgoing, offering each person she saw a loving smile or a kind word. When we got to Nana's room, she said loudly, "Hi, Nana, it's Wendy. I've come to sing to you." Then she pulled her guitar from its case and started playing and singing very tenderly to her.

My tight shoulders slowly released their grip on my neck, and my discomfort melted away as I allowed myself to open up to the river of love flowing from this twenty-two-year-old woman for her 105-year-old mother's mother's mother. *What is happening here?* I thought. *What am I witnessing? What kind of young person graduates from college and, rather than exploring the world and exploiting the freedom of singleness, chooses this?* I was overwhelmed, pierced straight through. *Love* is what I was witnessing. Wendy knew how to love people in a way I wanted and needed to learn. That's when I knew I'd be crazy ever to let this woman out of my life.

Sadly, as I shared earlier, the very thing that so attracted me to Wendy also threatened me on another level. Slowly but surely, our marriage would reveal to me how layers of fear, pride, and arrogance had crippled me in my ability to love. All those lessons in being just as cool as I was that I imposed on my wife came, just as Pope Francis says, from my own puffed-up sense of knowledge and self-importance. But I've been shamed in my arrogance again and again as the gospel logic of "the first shall be last and the last shall be first" has played itself out in my life.

The plain truth of the matter is that *I* was the one who in so many ways was uncool. Although I would need to relearn these lessons repeatedly (old patterns of thinking die hard), somehow I intuited the truth of the matter when I saw Wendy loving her nana. Underneath the facade of my own arrogance I realized that what "really makes us important," as Pope Francis says, "is a love that understands, shows concern, and embraces the weak."

Lord, how can I embrace the weak when I often loathe my own weaknesses and hide them behind masks of having it together? Free me from the lies that see weakness as something unlovable, something to be rejected. Teach me to love!

The gospel teaches us that the first shall be last and the last shall be first. How do I live out this logic in my own life? How do I deal with my own arrogance and pride when it crops up?

What are some of the hidden (or not so hidden) ways in which I consider myself superior to others?

How do I feel about myself when my weaknesses are on display? What is my attitude toward others when I observe their weaknesses?

It is important for Christians to show their love by the way they treat family members who are less knowledgeable about the faith, weak or less sure in their convictions. At times the opposite occurs: the supposedly mature believers within the family become unbearably arrogant. Love, on the other hand, is marked by humility; if we are to understand, forgive and serve others from the heart, our pride has to be healed and our humility must increase. (98)

Ugh! This memory makes me cringe. I was twenty-two years old, a fairly new and overzealous revert to my faith. My eighteen-year-old sister was going through a really difficult time in her life, and she and I had already had various clashes when it came to matters of faith. It's not that she didn't have faith. She had a very deep faith—a faith, in fact, more mature than mine, as I would later come to see, because it had been tested by deep suffering.

But it didn't line up with what I in my rigid thinking at the time considered proof of "real" faith.

My dad and I were trying without success to console my sister in her suffering one day and I muttered, "I think your problem is you just don't know God." Man, did she let me have it! And my dad took her side, challenging me quite directly on my unbearable arrogance. It was a wake-up call for me: If I was to understand and serve my sister from the heart, my pride had to be healed, just as Pope Francis says, and I had to be humbled.

Love is not arrogant. Sometimes I am. Lord, teach me to love!

Have I ever allowed pride to encroach on my otherwise sincere desire to witness to the faith? If so, how can I humble myself before those I may have wounded?

How can I cultivate genuine humility in my dealings with others?

SIX

Love Is Not Rude

To love is also to be gentle and thoughtful. . . . [L]ove is not rude or impolite; it is not harsh. Its actions, words and gestures are pleasing and not abrasive or rigid. (99)

My heart sank as I read the headline in the campus newspaper: "Rude Man with a Bible Confronts Gay Fellowship." Yikes! I was the man.

I was a junior at the University of Maryland. It was the time of year when all the campus groups and clubs had their tables on display in the student center. The day before the headline appeared I had been walking from table to table and came upon a display that read "UMD Gay Fellowship." New again to my faith and overzealous (as I already mentioned), I thought it was my duty to evangelize these people right away. So I pulled my Bible out of my backpack and . . . it all went downhill from there.

First words out of my mouth (in a very superior, judgmental tone): "Do you know what the Bible says about your lifestyle?" The young guys behind the table rolled their eyes as if to say, "Oh boy, another religious nutcase." One of them, an effeminate African-American guy, came out from behind the table to engage me in conversation. At one point during our strained exchange, he placed his hand on my shoulder. "Don't touch me!" I snapped, pulling away from him as if he were carrying some contagious disease. It was pure bravado intended to boost my own fragile sense of masculine identity in the face of his effeminacy—my rudeness nothing but a cover-up of my own fears and insecurities.

Dear Lord, wherever that man is now, please, somehow, if it is possible, let him know how deeply I regret the way I treated him that day. I was a very poor witness to you. Please forgive me. Somewhere beneath my fears, insecurities, and misguided zeal, there was a desire to bring healing, to witness to the truth about love. If anything, my superior attitude and rude actions only deepened the hurt and the wounds.

> ## Love is not rude. Sometimes I am.
> ## Lord Jesus, have mercy on me, a sinner.
>
> ---
>
> When I react rudely or impolitely toward others, what's getting tapped inside me? Anger? Fear? Insecurity? Disappointment? And what might be at the root of those feelings? Where do they come from?
>
> How do I respond when someone is rude to me?

[T]he deeper love is, the more it calls for respect for the other's freedom and the ability to wait until the other opens the door to his or her heart. (99)

These words of Pope Francis remind me of a very important teaching from St. John Paul II's Theology of the Body, drawn from this evocative line in the Song of Songs: "A garden locked is my sister, my bride, a garden locked, a fountain sealed" (4:12). While John Paul II explores both of these metaphors—"garden locked" and "fountain sealed"—primarily in connection with the truth about marital love and sexual union, we can extend the important lessons learned in that regard to the more general point Pope Francis is making.

Both metaphors convey the deeply personal meaning of sexual union, according to John Paul II. In particular, they speak with profound reverence of the mystery of femininity and the love with which a husband must approach his wife's "garden"—both the garden of her heart and the garden of her womb. Initially, her garden is "locked" and her fountain "sealed" as a clear sign of the woman's self-possession. She is "master of her own mystery," as John Paul II expressed it. And that means the woman holds the key to her own garden, which remains closed until she alone wills to open it.

Recognizing this, the bridegroom in the Song of Songs knows he cannot take her or grasp her. He, of course, *longs* with all his being to enter her mystery, her heart, her garden: "Open to me, my sister, my love, my dove, my perfect one; for my head is wet with dew" (5:2). But he knows, as Pope Francis reminds us, that love calls for respect for the other's freedom and the ability to wait until the other opens the door. If the man were to barge into this enclosed garden (in thought or deed), or if he were to manipulate her into surrendering the key, he would not be loving her; he would be violating her, using her, asserting himself as master over her. And persons, precisely as persons, must never be mastered. It's an intrinsic violation of their dignity.

This is not so for dogs, horses, or elephants. Of course, we hope Fido's master isn't cruel, but simply to place oneself as master over an animal is not a violation of that animal, whereas it is for a person. Why? Because as persons we are our own agents, the masters of our own decisions. No one can substitute his or her will for mine without encroaching on and violating my turf. Someone might very much want me to want what he wants, but no one can want *for* me, and no one can force me to want what he wants. This is where the impassable limit between persons, dictated by the dignity of free will, becomes clear.

In marriage, as in all human relationships, it often happens that one person wants the other to want what he or she wants. Conflict between spouses can be felt in a particular way regarding sexual desires. Pope Francis observes that "within marriage itself, sex can become a source of suffering and manipulation. Hence [Pope Paul VI's teaching] must be clearly reaffirmed that 'a conjugal act imposed on one's spouse without regard to his or her condition, or personal and reasonable wishes in the matter, is no true act of love . . .'" (*The Joy of Love,* 154).

At different times in our marriage, both Wendy and I have felt the other's lack of love in dealing with conflicting desires—whether they be specifically sexual or any number of other desires. It is never easy to face and work through the underlying issues rooted in our differences (and often our fallen humanity) from which these conflicts spring. One thing that has helped me tremendously in dealing with them is learning how to release Wendy from the burden of being my perfect fulfillment. There is an ache in every human being for love, for union, for affirmation, for life and joy that God and only God can fulfill. As a sacrament, marriage is meant to be a sign or icon of that definitive fulfillment, but it is not meant to *be* that definitive fulfillment. When we demand a spouse fill the void that only God can fill, the icon becomes an idol.

I know my own idolatry in this regard has been a source of great tension and struggles in my marriage. Those struggles have decreased in the measure that Wendy and I have learned what Pope Francis calls "the principle of spiritual realism" in marriage—the interior freedom to release the other person from the burden of completely satisfying my needs. "Each day we have to invoke the help of the Holy Spirit to make this interior freedom possible," says Pope Francis. This does not mean denying or repressing our needs; rather, it means learning how to open them to God in prayer (see *The Joy of Love*, 320). For prayer, the fathers of the Church tell us, is nothing but becoming a longing for God.

Love respects the freedom of others.
Love does not expect more from others
than they can provide. Sometimes I do.
Lord, teach me to love.

Am I impatient, demanding, or domineering in seeking
what *I* want in my relationships? Do I fail to respect the
freedom of others because their desires conflict with mine?

In what ways have I turned to human relationships to
fill the void in me that only God can fill?

To be open to a genuine encounter with others, "a kind look" is essential. This is incompatible with a negative attitude that readily points out other people's shortcomings while overlooking one's own. A kind look helps us to see beyond our own limitations, to be patient and to cooperate with others . . . (100)

No one who flies regularly can help but notice that the agents who check IDs and usher passengers through security have a rather unrewarding job to do. They're often the object of frustrated travelers' scorn and derision. I get it. They're an easy target, and I'm not immune to copping a negative attitude, especially when I'm late for a flight and security just selected me for additional screening.

How can we remain open in such frustrating circumstances to a genuine encounter with others? Here's a suggestion: Next time you hand your ID to one of those overworked and underappreciated agents, offer a kind look—a smile, even a word of gratitude. Or the next time security pulls you aside to check your bag or pat you down, instead of groaning and rolling your eyes (been there), say a kind word like, "Hey, thanks for keeping us safe." I think you'll be amazed at the goodwill it creates.

Love calls me to overcome my negative
attitudes toward others. Sometimes I prefer
to hang on to them. Lord, teach me to love.

Who are the random people I encounter in the course of a week? How can I remain open to a genuine encounter with them?

What can I do to foster such encounters, and what attitudes in me hinder them?

SEVEN

Love Does Not Insist on Its Own Way

Paul's hymn to love . . . states that love "does not seek its own interest," nor "seek what is its own." This same idea is expressed in another text: "Let each of you look not only to his own interests, but also to the interests of others" (Phil 2:4). (101)

I love food. It's amazing how possessive I can be at the dinner table about *that* particular piece of lasagna (you know, the one with just the right amount of perfectly melted cheese on top) or *that* particular serving of my wife's apple crisp (you know, the one with all the extra cinnamon-delicious crumbles on top). Thing is, 95 percent of the time, one or more of my children has his or her eye on the very same serving *I* want.

As a little way of looking out for the interests of others, I try to let my kids have dibs. My eye still instinctively falls on the piece of chicken *I'd* like, and almost inevitably there's a little tug-of-war inside when one of my kids reaches for it. But I know those little deaths are good for me. They're necessary, in fact, if I want to grow in what it means to love.

Love does not insist on its own way, nor demand its own interest. Lord, sometimes I fight letting go and deferring to others. Teach me how to love.

In what ways, little or large, am I quick to assert my own interests and override the interests of others?

What "little death" can I commit myself to in order to show concern for the interests of others?

[L]ove can transcend and overflow the demands of justice, "expecting nothing in return" (Lk 6:35), and the greatest of loves can lead to "laying down one's life" for another (cf. Jn 15:13). Can such generosity, which enables us to give freely and fully, really be possible? Yes, because it is demanded by the gospel. (102)

There's a distinction between love as desire and love as benevolence. If love as desire says, "I long for you *as* a good," love as benevolence says, "I long for *your* good; I long for that which is good for you."

Love as desire is not itself a problem or a defect, but it is incomplete. It must be balanced with love as benevolence for love to be fully itself. Speaking of marital love in particular, Pope Francis observed that it "cannot be seen purely as generous donation and self-sacrifice, where each spouse renounces all personal needs and seeks only the other's good without concern for personal satisfaction. We need to remember that authentic love also needs to be able to receive the other, to accept one's own vulnerability and needs, and to welcome with sincere and joyful gratitude the physical expressions of love found in a caress, an embrace, a kiss and sexual union" (*The Joy of Love*, 157).

Still, the person who truly loves longs not only for his or her own good, but for the other person's good, and he or she does so with no ulterior motive, no selfish consideration. This is "the greatest of loves," as Pope Francis says, and it also brings the greatest interior joy.

I'll always remember the day I realized Wendy loved me with this kind of disinterested benevolence. Even after my experience of her love for her great-grandmother, it caught me so deeply by surprise that I could barely believe it was real.

Wendy and I were part of the same group of friends in our college years. I had no idea, however, that over the course of about three years she had been hoping and praying one day I would be her husband. My obliviousness to Wendy's interest in me was due in part to the fact that during those same years I was interested in another person in the group, Laura. Various external factors (mainly her father) kept Laura and me from ever dating officially, and the whole tangled affair had caused me a lot of pain.

Wendy and I were getting more serious, and she once asked me why Laura and I had never dated. I was very reluctant to say anything about it, for I had just learned how interested Wendy had been in me the whole time I was interested in Laura. I was certain, based on my experience with other women, that sharing the story with Wendy would only make her insecure, jealous, and upset. But she seemed so sincere in her desire to know about it that I ended up sharing the whole painful saga.

Sure enough, she got all teary and emotional. *I knew it!* I thought to myself. *I never should have told her!* Then, to my utter astonishment, as Wendy opened up to me, I realized that her tears were for *me*—that she was feeling *my* pain. She went on to tell me that for some time she had known that something was preventing Laura and me from dating, so she had been praying that whatever the obstacle was, it would be removed and Laura and I would be able to pursue a relationship with each other as we desired.

I couldn't believe my ears. *"What?* . . . Run that by me again. . . . You're telling me that you were hoping to marry me for all that time, but when you found out Laura and I wanted to be together but couldn't be, you started praying that she and I would get together?"

"Yes," she said. "Wasn't that what you wanted?"

"Yes," I replied, "but why did *you* want that for me?"

"Because love means you lay down your life and your own desires for the good of the other," she said.

I had never experienced such a selfless love from a woman who was romantically interested in me. I was utterly flabbergasted. Six and a half months later she was my wife.

> Love calls me to a generosity that gives freely and fully, without expecting anything in return.

Sometimes I'm focused only on myself and my personal preferences, desires, and comforts. Lord, teach me to love.

Why do I find it difficult to sacrifice my own way for others? Am I concerned that my desires will be left unsatisfied or unfulfilled if I do not insist on my own way at least some of the time?

How does the gospel paradox of "dying in order to live" play itself out in my life and in my relationships? Do I profess belief in the gospel, but then make choices to the contrary? How? And why?

What are some ways I can choose to give up my own way this week?

EIGHT

Love Is Not Irritable

[An] interior indignation . . . a hidden irritation . . . sets us on edge where others are concerned, as if they were troublesome or threatening and thus to be avoided. To nurture such interior hostility helps no one. It only causes hurt and alienation. (103)

I've sung my wife's praises. Now, in order to confess another fault of my own, I must bring to light one of hers. As she readily admits, she's a procrastinator. And sometimes it's rather irritating to a do-it-and-get-it-done kind of guy like me.

Here's one example: I unpack my suitcase as soon as I get home from a trip. Wendy's suitcase might sit in our room for days untouched. Here's what goes on in my head when I walk by that un-unpacked suitcase, if I'm not guarding myself:

- Day 1: She was tired last night when we got home. She'll get to it when she's able.
- Day 2: She must have had a hard day with the kids. She'll probably get to it tonight.
- Day 3: There's really no excuse today. She's just not getting to it. What is her deal?

- Day 4: What is she thinking when she walks by this suitcase every day—*Maybe I'll get to it next week?*
- Day 5: Does she just think this thing is going to unpack itself? It only would have taken five minutes when we got home the other night to unpack this darned thing. Why doesn't she just think (and behave) like me? Life would be much easier if she did.

By this time my little weed of interior irritation is not so little. Rather than uprooting it the moment it sprouted, as I should have done, I've been watering it. And watered weeds of irritation inevitably become subtle or maybe not-so-subtle attacks on my wife's person: *Why doesn't she just think (and behave) like me?* That seems like an easy way out of my irritation, but in the end, it would be my loss. As Pope Francis observes, "The combination of two different ways of thinking can lead to a synthesis that enriches both. The unity that we seek is not uniformity, but a unity in diversity,' or 'reconciled diversity.' . . . We need to free ourselves from feeling that we all have to be alike" (*The Joy of Love*, 139).

"A persistently critical attitude towards one's spouse," he says later, "is a sign that marriage was not entered into as a project to be worked on together, with patience, understanding, tolerance and generosity" (218).

I take comfort in knowing that saints are not ready-made heroes of virtue. Like the rest of us, they have to struggle to acquire virtue. St. Thérèse of Lisieux, for example, writes in her autobiography about the "clicking noises" that a sister in her community made when sitting behind her during times of meditation. "[I]t would be impossible for me to tell you how much this little noise wearied me," she admitted. Who can't relate? Thérèse, however, learned to offer her irritation as a prayer to grow in love toward this person.

Love is not irritable. Sometimes I am. Lord, teach me to love.

What are the things others do in my life that irritate me? How can I turn that irritation into an opportunity to grow in love for the person irritating me?

What do I think I will accomplish by watering the weeds of irritation instead of uprooting them? What hidden satisfaction do I find in doing so?

It is one thing to sense a sudden surge of hostility and another to give in to it, letting it take root in our hearts: "Be angry but do not sin; do not let the sun go down on your anger" (Eph 4:26). My advice is never to let the day end without making peace in the family. And how am I going to make peace? By getting down on my knees? No! Just by a small gesture, a little something, and harmony within your family will be restored. (104)

Sometimes when Wendy and I are lying in bed knowing that some interaction left us both irritated earlier in the day, I'll reach out and put my hand on her shoulder to let her know I love her.

She'll do the same. And we both know we're loved. Little things sometimes are not so little.

> Love invites small gestures of kindness and affection. Sometimes I struggle even to offer a little something. Lord, teach me to love.
>
> _____
>
> What little efforts or gestures can I make to restore harmony in my wounded relationships?
>
> What are some peaceful ways I can end the day with my loved ones so anger doesn't gain a foothold?

Our first reaction when we are annoyed should be one of heartfelt blessing, asking God to bless, free and heal that person. "On the contrary bless, for to this you have been called, that you may obtain a blessing" (1 Peter 3:9). (104)

I was a pretty angry teenager. If someone cut me off in traffic, one way or another I'd let that inconsiderate driver know how peeved I was.

In my early twenties, I had a fairly dramatic experience of coming to faith in Christ. One of the certain proofs that something was truly different inside me was when someone cut me off in traffic and I responded with, "God bless that guy; he must be late for something."

What? *Where did that come from?* I thought to myself. Somebody had been rearranging the furniture in my heart.

Love calls me to offer heartfelt blessing to those who annoy me. Sometimes, I'd prefer to see heads roll. Lord, teach me to love.

If we find it difficult to bless those who annoy us (which is to say, to love those who annoy us), the remedy is not just to try harder, but to open ourselves more deeply to God's love for us. We can't give what we don't have. "In this is love, not that we loved God but that he loved us" (1 John 4:10). In what areas of my own life do I need to open up to God's transforming love?

What does it mean to bless someone who annoys me?

NINE

Love Is Not Resentful

The opposite of resentment is forgiveness, which is rooted in a positive attitude that seeks to understand other people's weaknesses and to excuse them. As Jesus said, "Father, forgive them; for they know not what they do" (Lk 23:34). . . . When we have been offended or let down, forgiveness is possible and desirable, but no one can say that it is easy. The truth is that family communion can only be preserved and perfected through a great spirit of sacrifice. It requires, in fact, a ready and generous openness of each and all to understanding, to forbearance, to pardon, to reconciliation. (105–106)

Remember my confession in the introduction about how clueless I was early in our marriage, and how I thought my ship had come in when I was offered that major book deal? Even more major was the wake-up call coming my way when Wendy heard the title. The biggest publishing house in the world had brought me to New York City, wined and dined me, and asked me to write a book for husbands called *Loving Her Rightly*.

Expecting my wife would rejoice with me at this great opportunity, I was rather stunned to see her face fall. "Honey, you and I need to talk," she said, "and it's gonna be long and it's gonna be painful." Everything in her face and body language was telling me loudly and clearly that I was in no place to be writing a book for husbands called *Loving Her Rightly*.

By the grace of God, maybe for the first time in ten years of marriage, I knew I really needed to listen to my wife. So, I decided not to pursue the book deal. Instead, over the course of several weeks, I let Wendy tell me what it had been like to be married to the "Theology of the Body guy." She was right—it was long and it was painful.

I don't want to paint the wrong picture. In fact, my wife has needed to remind me of the ways I had always been open to growing in our marriage. We're all made up of wheat and weeds. There was a lot of wheat in our marriage, but there were also plenty of weeds, and I was conveniently ignoring some pretty big ones. It's one thing to have lots of good theology *about* God's plan for man and woman in your head, and it's another thing to *live* it. It's one thing to write books, give lectures, and teach classes on the meaning of love, and it's another thing to walk through the painful purifications that are an absolutely necessary part of the journey of learning *how* to love. Praise God for his mercy, and for my wife's!

As Pope Francis says, family communion requires a generous openness to understanding, to forbearance, and to forgiveness. But this does *not* mean sweeping pain under the rug or trying really hard to forget how others may have hurt us. The *Catechism of the Catholic Church* puts it plainly: "It is not in our power not to feel or to forget an offense . . ." What, then, are we to do with the pain? The *Catechism* goes on to say that "the heart that offers itself to the Holy Spirit turns injury into compassion and purifies the memory in transforming the hurt into intercession" (2843). There are a few different layers to this. Let's take a look.

First, forgiveness does not mean saying, "It's okay." If it were okay, there'd be no reason to ask for forgiveness. In order to forgive, we must open our hearts to a love that does not originate in us. We must open our pain to the very love of God. If we do, that divine spirit of love promises to transform our injury into compassion. To feel compassion means "to suffer with." Why did that person cause us pain? Because that person also was in pain; someone else had caused him or her similar pain. This means we now *know* that person's pain—because, in a very real way, we feel it ourselves. And knowing just how pained the person is who caused us pain is the key to having our injury turned into compassion.

Second, when we open our hearts to the true Spirit of forgiveness, he purifies the memory. It's not that the memory disappears, but it no longer stings in the same way. When the memory presents itself, it need no longer be a re-wounding or a rehashing of anger and resentment. In fact, the memory itself can become a healing prayer, both for us and for the person who wounded us.

This, finally, is what the *Catechism* means when it says that the Holy Spirit can transform our hurt into intercession: "Father, forgive them; for they know not what they do" (Luke 23:34). The pain itself, offered and opened to God, just as Christ did on the cross, becomes intercession for the person who wounded us; it becomes a truly effective means of furthering Christ's redemption in the world, for it is a profoundly intimate experience of union with Jesus in his suffering.

I know this is real. This is what my wife did for me. Had she just come at me with anger and resentment for the pain I had caused her, I would probably have gone into defensive mode. Instead, I could tell that in sharing the reality of her pain with me, she had learned the art of offering that pain as a prayer *for me*. Through her I have come to learn in profoundly life-altering ways what it means to say the Lord is kind and merciful.

Forgiveness is not cheap. Its price is clear in the crucifixion of our Lord. The call to follow Christ is the call to enter into *his* manner of loving, a manner of loving willing to take on others' pain and offer it in intercession. It does not come from us. It is not in our power. Even the ability to surrender to this power is not in our power.

> All is grace. All is gift. All is mercy.
> Jesus, grant us the grace to open all of our
> pain to this power. Amen.

Who has caused me the most pain in my life?
Has it ever dawned on me that those who have caused
me this pain are in similar pain?

What has prevented me from allowing my pain to
become compassion and intercession for the person
who caused me this pain?

If we have been the innocent victim of another's pain,
we can feel forgotten by God. In our own sense of
abandonment, whether we realize it or not, we are deeply
united with Christ in his cry from the cross:
"My God, my God, why have you abandoned me?"

*Write a letter to God expressing the deepest agony of
your heart and asking him to transform it.*

**Today we recognize that being able to forgive others implies
the liberating experience of understanding and forgiving
ourselves. (107)**

Why do we often find forgiving ourselves even more difficult than
forgiving others? I know it's necessary to forgive myself for the
ways I screw up, break faith with God, hurt myself, and wound
others—but something in me resists. For some odd reason, I often
prefer to condemn myself rather than forgive myself. As with
Inspector Javert from *Les Misérables,* something in me prefers cold
justice to mercy, even if it means inflicting it on myself.

My confessor has pointed out to me that I like to think this
is a virtue, when in fact it is pure vice. He's helped me realize
that self-condemnation is one of the twin towers of sin in my life.
The other is self-reliance. In this regard, I'm a practical atheist.
I confess belief in God (and that I'm not he), but practically
speaking, part of me likes to think I don't need him. I like to think
I'm in control of my own life and my own salvation. So I rely
on myself to "get it right," and then when I inevitably fail, I beat
myself up for the fact that my self-reliance wasn't, in fact, reliable.

That, I think, is what really bugs me about forgiving myself:
To forgive myself is to admit way down inside that my lifelong
project of self-reliance has been utterly futile. And part of me
doesn't want to throw in the towel. Even if my self-judgment is

harsher than God's, part of me prefers to judge myself because it's still *my* judgment, and that keeps me in control; that keeps me as the god of my own life. It seems that somewhere inside I want to reserve the ability to condemn myself because logically it's the flip side of another ability I want to reserve: the ability to save myself. It's called P-R-I-D-E.

"In the gospel the very root of sin," observes theologian Olivier Clément, "is the pretense that we can save ourselves by our own effort." We have leaned so heavily on our own supposed ability to please God that for "a moment we must lose our balance," according to Clément; we "must see in a flash of clarity . . . the ripping apart of our protective covering of happiness or moral virtue." If we allow ourselves to be stripped in this way, it will draw out of us "a cry of trust and love *de profundis*, from the depths of the heart." And from the depths of our hearts, we'll be able to forgive ourselves for wishing we didn't need God.

> Lord, forgive me for not forgiving myself. Teach me to love, understand, and forgive myself so that I can do the same for others.

Do I find it hard to forgive myself? If so, why? What am I clinging to? Why do I prefer to be harsher with myself than God is?

In what ways am I a practical atheist, preferring self-reliance to relying entirely on God? In what ways am I still trying to save myself or, on the flip side, condemn myself?

In your own words, ask God for the grace to recognize the futility of your self-reliance (pride) and to embrace peacefully your need for him ("Apart from me you can do nothing," as Jesus said).

Often our mistakes, or criticism we have received from loved ones, can lead to a loss of self-esteem. We become distant from others, avoiding affection and fearful in our interpersonal relationships. Blaming others becomes falsely reassuring. We need to learn to pray over our past history, to accept ourselves, to learn how to live with our limitations, and even to forgive ourselves, in order to have this same attitude towards others. (107)

I have come in my adult years to understand some of the roots of my need to be "cool" as a kid. It came slowly and sometimes painfully by learning to pray over my "past history," as Pope Francis says we need to do.

I was probably in my late thirties when I had this trigger experience. At a family gathering my older brother looked at me from across the room and mockingly imitated the way I was chewing on a pretzel. The rage that welled up inside me was far out of proportion to the offense. Something got tapped, and from years of spiritual direction, I knew this was the kind of thing that I needed to look at prayerfully.

The next day I wrote in my prayer journal, "Lord, shine your light on that rage that welled up in my heart last night." As I tried to listen attentively, it wasn't long before a flood of memories from childhood were parading through my mind—all of them occasions when my older brother mocked me for this or that (especially when my quirks, weaknesses, and imperfections were on display). And then the tapes started replaying: "You're a dork!" "Don't be such a dork!" *Dork* was definitely my brother's insult of choice when we were kids.

Over several weeks of allowing God's light into those memories, I started to see how my brother's insults had impacted me. At first, I didn't really want to admit that they had gone that deep. I mean, it wasn't *that* bad. It was just normal older brother stuff, right? Other tapes started playing in my head: "You're such a wuss. Get over it!" Whenever we hear messages in our heads like that, it's important to ask ourselves whose voice it is. Is that what God would say? No. In fact, it was my loving Father who was shining his light on my pain and encouraging me to bring it out into the open so he could heal it. It was some other voice that was wanting me to keep it buried.

Praying over my history eventually took me to a moment in my childhood when, as a way of coping with the barrage of insults, I resolved internally that if couldn't beat him, I'd join him. It was a survival mechanism—to survive the insults, I had to agree with them, because resisting them seemed hopeless when I was a kid. My goal from that moment on became winning my brother's approval, and he was one of the cool kids. I started wearing masks that I thought made me lovable, all the while haunted by the realization that wearing these masks was itself an admission of my worst fear—that, in fact, underneath it all, I am what the insults say I am: an unlovable dork.

Precisely what Pope Francis says can happen to those criticized by loved ones happened to me: I became distant from others, avoiding affection and fearful in my interpersonal relationships. Blaming others became falsely reassuring. I needed (and still need) to learn how to pray over my past history, to love and accept myself as I really am—quirks, imperfections, and all. I needed (and still need) to learn how to live with my limitations, and to forgive myself for accepting the "verdict" of my brother's insults. And I've needed (and still need) to learn how to extend this same attitude toward others, beginning with my older brother.

I've had to work through a lot of resentment toward him. Why did he cause me so much pain? I've come to see it's because he was in pain. That's the beginning of compassion. That's the beginning of learning how to offer my pain as intercession. Each of us, as Pope Francis observes, is "an unfinished product, needing to grow, a work in progress" (*The Joy of Love*, 218). To the degree that we accept that about ourselves and love ourselves there, we can accept that about others and love them there—even when they've caused us a great deal of pain.

Love is not resentful. Sometimes I am.
Lord, teach me to love.

What were my relationships with loved ones (parents, siblings, cousins) like as I was growing up?
Was I loved unconditionally in my mistakes, foibles, and weaknesses, or was I ridiculed or harshly criticized?

> Whom in my family of origin do I need to forgive for failing to love me as I am?
>
> *In your own words, ask God for the grace to learn what it means to pray over your past history. Ask him to shine his light on ways that you may have become distant from others, avoiding affection because of certain fears.*

All [that I've said about showing love and mercy to others] assumes that we ourselves have had the experience of being forgiven by God, justified by his grace and not by our own merits. [It assumes we] have known a love that is prior to any of our own efforts, a love that constantly opens doors, promotes and encourages. If we accept that God's love is unconditional . . . then we will become capable of showing boundless love and forgiving others [who] have wronged us. (108)

As I said in the introduction, I believe this assumption from Pope Francis takes us to the very heart of who he is, what he believes, and what he is trying to teach the Church and the world: God's unconditional love is the foundation of absolutely *everything* the Church is; hence, it is the fundamental gift the Church has to share with the world. Each of us is a beggar before God, with a gaping, aching need for what only he can give us. That's threatening only if God is a tyrant with whom we must win favor in order to receive measly crumbs from his table. But if God *is* love, if God *is* a gift, and if the gift he gives is *himself*, then we needn't hide or reject our need before him. We need only open it, trusting that we will be "filled with all the fullness of God" (Ephesians 3:19). Life then becomes praise and thanksgiving for his love, for his gift.

Have we truly opened our need to the astounding gift of God's unconditional love, or are we still striving somehow to increase our divine approval rating? One way of examining our consciences here is to ask how loving and merciful we are toward others. Are we quick to look down on those who do not think and behave as we do? If so, chances are we secretly think we've won some special favor with God through our own merits.

In the Church's wisdom, when the Gospel story of the "sinful" woman who weeps at the Lord's feet appears in the cycle of readings, it's coupled with St. Paul's teaching that a person "is not justified by works of the law but through faith in Jesus Christ" (Galatians 2:16). Faith in Jesus, as St. John Paul II explained, is the openness of the human heart to God's gift—the humble opening of our gaping need for love to the infinite supply flowing from the gaping heart of the crucified Christ. If we're trying to justify ourselves, however, "then Christ died to no purpose" (Galatians 2:21).

When the sinful woman crashes the party at Simon's house, humbly opening her need before Jesus, Simon swells with pride and says indignantly, "If this man were a prophet, he would have known who and what sort of woman this is who is touching him . . ." (Luke 7:39). After telling the short parable of the two debtors, one who owed much and one who owed little, Jesus turns to the woman and asks Simon a simple but penetrating question: "Do you see this woman?" (Luke 7:44). Simon didn't *see* her. He *couldn't* see her. He was blinded by his own presumed ability to please God, which he believed gave him the right to look down on those he assumed didn't please God.

We need only call to mind the parable of the Pharisee and the tax collector praying in the temple to realize that our typical assessment of what justifies us before God is not God's assessment (see Luke 18:9–14). We have no reason to believe the Pharisee was lying about his "righteous deeds" when he delighted that he was not like the tax collector. His collection of righteous deeds, however, became a source of pride that blinded him to his utter need and poverty before God. And if you, like me, have found yourself being harsh with the Pharisee in this parable ("Well, thank God I'm not like that Pharisee who looks down on others"), aren't you, like me, guilty of looking down on him?

Mercy. We are *all* in need of it. And that's precisely the point: We're all in the same boat, and in case you haven't noticed, it's sinking. Only God's mercy can save us. We may well admit that that is the case, but it remains mere lip service if we still reserve the right to distance ourselves from those "really bad" sinners (be they of the pharisaical or licentious variety).

What's my paradigm? Unconditional love and forgiveness, or love *if* . . . forgiveness *if* . . . ? If what? If I'm worthy of it? If I perform well? If I'm not really *that* bad? Whenever I catch myself trying to justify myself by my own merits, I can be sure that somewhere in my heart I don't really believe in God's unconditional love. If I did, I wouldn't be striving so hard to earn it. As Pope Francis observes, if I accept that God's love for me is unconditional, then I'll become capable of showing that same boundless love and forgiveness to others.

God's love is unconditional. Often mine is not.
Lord, teach me to love as you love.

Do I have an attitude of entitlement when it comes to
deserving God's love and approval? If so, how does this
affect the way I view others?

Pope Francis admitted that sometimes, when he has seen a
person trying to justify himself "with so much outward rigidity,"
he has asked the Lord: "Throw down a banana peel in front
of him, so he takes a good slip, is ashamed of being a sinner,
and thus encounters you, who are the Savior." What are the
"banana peels" the Lord has sent in my life to humble me and
lead me to encounter Christ as my only salvation?

TEN

Love Does Not Rejoice at Wrong, but Rejoices in the Right

The expression *chairei epì te adikia* has to do with a negativity lurking deep within a person's heart. It is the toxic attitude of those who rejoice at seeing an injustice done to others. The following phrase expresses its opposite: *sygchairei te aletheia*: "it rejoices in the right." In other words, we rejoice at the good of others when we see their dignity and value their abilities and good works. (109)

I recently read that the world's largest porn site gets 2.4 million visitors per hour. In one year alone, people around the world watched 4.4 billion hours of its content—that's more than half a million years' worth . . . on only one of the millions of pornographic websites available. The magnitude of the problem and the misery it causes is simply unfathomable.

Why do I bring this up here? Because taking pleasure in the sexual exploitation of men and women in pornography is a keen example of "the toxic attitude of those who rejoice at seeing an injustice done to others." What could be more unjust to a person than turning a blind eye to his or her dignity and value by treating that person as an object to be exploited, used, bought, and sold for others' lustful gratification? And it is no less an injustice when such people seem to be willingly handing themselves over to be used and objectified in this way.

The way we overcome rejoicing at wrong, however, is not merely by condemning the wrong, but by rejoicing in the right. In this case, overcoming the wrong of pornography does not happen by negating sexuality and erotic desire; rather, it happens by coming to rejoice in God's glorious plan for them. As Pope Francis rightly insists, "the rejection of distortions of sexuality and eroticism should never lead us to a disparagement or neglect of sexuality and *eros* in themselves." To the degree that eros is rightly ordered, "it becomes a 'pure unadulterated affirmation' revealing the marvels of which the human heart is capable" (*The Joy of Love*, 157, 152).

The key here, of course, is rightly ordering our desires. Pope Francis speaks passionately about this need and this real possibility throughout his document on the family: "A person can certainly channel his passions in a beautiful and healthy way," he insists, "increasingly pointing them towards altruism and an integrated self-fulfillment" (148). The discipline required here involves "not the denial or destruction of desire so much as its broadening and perfection" (149).

One of the things God wants to show us is that behind all our misdirected desires and lusts, there is a legitimate desire he put there and wants to satisfy. Uncovering that legitimate desire and entrusting its satisfaction entirely to God is critical to our healing and wholeness. Father Jacques Philippe makes this point insightfully when he observes that "one passion can only be cured by another—a misplaced love by a greater love, wrong behavior by right behavior that makes provisions for the desire underlying the wrongdoing, recognizes the conscious or unconscious needs that seek fulfillment and . . . offers them legitimate satisfaction." Some people call this "inner healing."

Here's an example from my own life. I was six or seven years old the first time I was exposed to pornography. In my teen years rejoicing in this wrong became a habit. When I gave my life to Christ in my early twenties, I was in need of serious healing from all the distorted images that had been ingrained in my mind. A few weeks before my wedding, I was in a chapel praying specifically that the Lord would make me a true gift to my bride on my wedding night. Right then and there I was bombarded by a stream of pornographic flashbacks, and I cried out to God for help. I heard a voice in my heart say, "Give all those lies to me and I will show you the truth you were really looking for." In my mind's eye I saw an image of a fire, and as I pulled all these pornographic images up and out of my heart and placed them into the fire, I prayed, "Lord, please untwist these lies and show me the truth."

To my astonishment, what emerged from the fire as the lies were consumed was an image so beautiful, so holy, and so healing it moved me to tears. It was an image of the Christ child nursing at the breast of the Blessed Mother. My heart cried out: "Yes, *that's* what I have been looking for the whole time—to be fed like the Christ child in this holy, beautiful way. Forgive me, Lord, for all the sinful ways I have acted out, not trusting that you desired to feed this deep hunger in my soul all along."

Would that that had been a definitive healing and the end of all of my disordered desires. Alas, the inner healing we need takes us on a lifelong journey that passes through various levels of painful interior purification. Step by step we learn to expose the real contents of our hearts to God and let him transform our desires. The more we do so, the more we mourn what is wrong and rejoice in what is right, even when what is right carries with it a heavy sacrifice.

Love does not rejoice at wrong. Sometimes I do. Lord, teach me to rejoice in the right. Teach me to love!

What is my honest attitude toward pornography—not the attitude I think I should have, but the attitude I actually have? How can I grow in rejoicing in the right of God's marvelous gift of the human body and human sexuality?

Have I ever invited God's healing light into my ideas and attitudes toward my own body and sexuality? What distorted or diseased ideas and images of the body and of sexuality am I in need of surrendering to the Lord?

In your own words, write a prayer asking Christ to untwist whatever sin has twisted in your heart and mind regarding the beauty and splendor of his plan for sexual love and union.

[Rejoicing in the right] is impossible for those who must always be comparing and competing . . . so that they secretly rejoice in [others'] failures. (109)

Comparing and competing—it's another symptom of "cool syndrome." Cool people have to be on top, have to have the upper hand, to be the best, to have the spotlight, to dominate. All of this has exterior manifestations, of course, but it's even more so an interior game. In their own minds and hearts, cool people maintain their own supposed coolness by secretly recognizing, labeling, and even rejoicing in the supposed uncoolness of others.

Who is being uncool here? Oh, the irony.

When I was a kid, this interior competition was mostly about the way people dressed, looked, and acted, and the kind of music they listened to. When, as an adult, I devoted my life to studying and teaching theology, the remnants of that same self-exalting habit became more about spiritual and theological matters. For example, I've caught myself taking a secret delight in detecting other people's theological errors. What is this sickness in us that, one way or another, wants to feel superior to others?

When we do this under the guise of religious matters, Pope Francis calls it "spiritual worldliness." From a posture of religious "accomplishment" and moral "success," the spiritually worldly person permits himself to look down on everyone else's failings, while utterly unaware that his own pride and lack of charity are "infinitely more disastrous," as Pope Francis asserts, than the failings he so readily condemns in others (see The Joy of the Gospel, 93). More often than not, the spiritually worldly person starts with sincere motives to live a devout life and to safeguard the Church's faith and doctrine. But, through pride, good devotion goes bad.

"Those who have fallen into [spiritual] worldliness," says Francis, "constantly point out the mistakes of others and they are obsessed by appearances. Their hearts are open only to the limited horizon of their own immanence and interests, and as a consequence they neither learn from their sins nor are they genuinely open to forgiveness. This is a tremendous corruption disguised as a good," concludes the Pope. Then he exclaims, "God save us from a worldly Church with superficial spiritual and pastoral trappings!" (*The Joy of the Gospel*, 97).

Love does not compare and compete in order to feel superior to others. Sometimes I do. Lord, teach me to love.

In what ways do I secretly (or not-so-secretly) compare myself with others and rejoice in their failings?

Am I quick to point out others' mistakes while hiding my own? What am I afraid of in having my mistakes on display?

Looking around at my world, what is one way I can rejoice in someone else's success or good fortune?

ELEVEN

Love Bears All Things

Paul says that love "bears all things" . . . This is about more than simply putting up with evil; it has to do with the use of the tongue. The verb can mean "holding one's peace" about what may be wrong with another person. It implies limiting judgment, checking the impulse to issue a firm and ruthless condemnation: "Judge not and you will not be judged" (Lk 6:37). (112)

Not long ago a close family friend came to dinner at our home. I'll call him Bob. There's been a history in our relationship of my not holding my peace with regard to ways in which Bob and I see the world differently. Although I firmly believe some of his views are damaging and wrong, there has been a history of *my* being in the wrong with Bob because of the immoderate use of my tongue when discussing those views. I've injured our relationship as a result.

Knowing Bob was coming over, I consciously prepped myself a bit so as *not* to fall into my pattern of losing my cool with him. So there we were at the table—my wife, my kids, and our friend Bob—and he started talking about the topic of looks and physical attractiveness in a way that is utterly contrary to everything I want my children to think about their own and other people's bodies. I responded initially with some calm challenges to his thinking, but as he persisted, I lost my cool and caused a scene. Something got tapped in me and up rose an impulse to issue a firm and rather ruthless condemnation of what he was saying. Despite my desire to do so, I did not check that impulse, as love demands I do. Instead, I let 'er rip.

I had a right to challenge what my friend was espousing in front of my children, but not in this ruthless way. In trying to spare my kids the bad example offered by my friend, I became a bad example myself. Mercy.

Love bears all things. Sometimes I find certain things unbearable and express myself in hurtful ways. Forgive me, Lord. Please, teach me to love.

In what ways have I failed to hold my peace and allowed my words to hurt others?

When someone is speaking inappropriately, how can I constructively and lovingly respond?

Being willing to speak ill of another person is a way of asserting ourselves, venting resentment and envy without concern for the harm we may do. We often forget that slander can be quite sinful; it is a grave offense against God when it seriously harms another person's good name and

causes damage that is hard to repair. . . . [L]ove cherishes the good name of others, even one's enemies. (112)

Okay, I get the principle—but how do I cherish the good name of others when they have not cherished mine? How do I love the person when I'm boiling with anger inside because of the way she's stabbed me in the back?

Recall the *Catechism's* teaching that "the heart that offers itself to the Holy Spirit turns injury into compassion and purifies the memory in transforming the hurt into intercession" (2843). I realize we looked at this in some detail earlier, but I know of no other way to love my enemies than "dying the death" that allows pain to become compassion, compassion to become prayer, and prayer to become love. This is not just a pious idea. It can become a reality, a lived experience, if we welcome the grace to enter into it.

Some years ago I was wrestling internally with someone who had slandered me. My spiritual director urged me to write out what I was really feeling and thinking in a letter to Jesus, without editing or censoring any of it. I did, and it felt *good* to get it out— really good! Then, in a kind of whisper I sensed in my heart, I felt Jesus saying to me, "The pain you feel is the pain this person feels. This person is pouring pain out on you because others have poured pain on this person. I'm asking you to bear this pain, to accept it freely, even welcome it for this person's sake. I'm asking you to suffer with this person and offer this pain as intercession for this person's healing. I'm asking you to love this person with me and through me and to allow me to love this person with you and through you."

Only a miracle of grace can transform the pain we feel into compassion for the people who caused us the pain, but I can attest that such miracles happen when we trust God enough to be open to his Spirit. The pain we feel can become prayer. And the prayer we offer can become love—in fact, it is itself love. Isn't this what Christ's death on the cross *is* in its very essence: pain experienced as compassion, offered as prayer, and expressed as love? When we enter into this miracle of grace and taste it, feel it, and experience it, it's no longer we who live, but Christ in us.

> We should expect miracles in learning to love. They happen. Lord, teach me how to remain open to them!

Have I spoken ill of people with a desire to cause them harm or to paint a negative picture of them in the minds of others? What were my hidden motivations for doing so? How can I make amends?

Do I need to forgive anyone who has spoken negatively of me?

Have I ever experienced a miracle of grace in my relationship with an "enemy"? How did God choose to work in this situation?

Far from ingenuously claiming not to see the problems and weaknesses of others, [love] sees those weaknesses and faults in a wider context. It recognizes that these failings are a part of a bigger picture. We have to realize that all of us are a complex mixture of light and shadows. The other person is much more than the sum of the little things that annoy me. (113)

I love Simon Peter. There's an irresistible realism we encounter in the paradox of his zeal and frailty. He's quick to get out of the boat, and just as quick to sink; quick to profess his loyalty to Christ, and quick to deny him. If you're like me, you've probably taken a lot of consolation in Peter's frailty, foibles, and sinfulness. And you may also have wondered what Jesus was thinking when he named *this* guy "the rock."

Jesus, of course, saw Peter's weaknesses and faults in a wider context. He knew what his power could do through Peter's weakness. And lest we fall into the error of idealizing the "post-Pentecost Peter," let us take to heart this important observation of Pope Benedict XVI: "We have grown accustomed to make a clear distinction between Peter the rock and Peter the denier of Christ—*the denier of Christ*: that is Peter as he was before Easter; *the rock*: that is Peter as he was after Pentecost, the Peter of whom we have constructed a singularly idealistic image. But, in reality, he was at both times both of these."

Holding the two together—rock *and* denier—can be a bit much for our wee brains. The either/or is much, much easier. Both/and creates tension, like that invisible force we feel when we try to hold together the opposing ends of two magnets. But it's right in that tension where we discover the truth about our humanity: Man is a "divided being," wrote Pope Benedict XVI, "pitiful in his greatness, yet still great while he is pitiful."

You already know, of course, that I'm a recovering perfectionist.

And the perfectionist believes he won't be loved until he rids himself of all pitifulness and gets his act together. Or, if I may say it just as my straight-talking spiritual director once said it to me: "Christopher, you think a saint is someone who has his shit together. No. You have it all wrong. A saint," he insisted, "is someone who has all his shit open to the merciful love of the Father."

Game changer.

If we let that sink in, it will forever destroy that false dichotomy of saints in one column and sinners in the other. Be honest. I bet, like me, you've kind of rolled your eyes whenever you've read the saints talking about what "wretched sinners" they are—*Yeah, sure you were, Mother Teresa. Whatever!* The more I've journeyed into intimacy with Jesus (which is to say the more I've journeyed into the depths of God's mercy, which is to say into the depths of my need for it), the more I've come to believe that these saints really were aware of how sinful they were. *That's* what made them saints: They didn't cover up their sinfulness with a pious mask; they didn't hide it behind self-righteous "accomplishments." They simply basked and bathed continually in God's mercy, trusting that their failings were part of a bigger picture.

When we know this about our own faults and failings, we know the same is true about others' faults and failings. This is what enables us to renounce every sense of superiority and all harsh judgments and simply learn to love other people—as Jesus loves them.

Jesus, please, please teach me how to bear all things, beginning with my own pitifulness.

Am I at peace with the fact that I'll always recognize weakness in myself and in others? If not, how can I realize that human weakness is part of a bigger, more beautiful picture that God already sees and is bringing to completion?

Do I place saints in one column and sinners in the other? What false notion of holiness does that betray? Am I striving for such false holiness?

What are the qualities of a true saint—and how does this differ from my preconceived notion of what sainthood looks like?

Love does not have to be perfect for us to value it. The other person loves me as best he can, with all his limits, but the fact that love is imperfect does not mean that it is untrue or unreal. It is real, albeit limited and earthly. If I expect too much, the other person will let me know, for he or she can neither play God nor serve all my needs. Love coexists with imperfection. It "bears all things" and can hold its peace before the limitations of the loved one. (113)

Some years ago Wendy and I were out to dinner and she observed that something was different about our marriage in recent years, something good. She asked me if I had any insight into what it was, and after reflecting a bit, I said with a smile, "Yeah, I think I know what it is. I think I've been realizing deep in my heart that you can't satisfy me." With a big smile on her face she said, "Yeah, *that's* it. And I've been realizing the same thing—you can't satisfy me either." I imagine anyone overhearing us in the restaurant thought we were about to get divorced, but to us that realization was cause for joy and celebration. We had never felt closer and freer in our love. Let me explain.

As Pope Francis affirms, we "urgently need to rediscover" how marriage points us to "the ultimate end and definitive dimension of our human existence." When this happens, "married couples will come to see the deeper meaning of their journey through this life" (*The Joy of Love*, 325). And here is that deeper meaning: Marriage in this life is meant to prepare us for the eternal marriage that awaits us in the next life—what Scripture calls "the marriage of the Lamb" (Revelation 19:7). And this means, as beautiful and fulfilling as human love can be, marriage is not our ultimate fulfillment. It is only a sign, an icon, a sacrament of the definitive love of God.

Wendy and I knew this in our heads when we got married, but our hearts were still in some ways *bent* toward each other, expecting and desiring the other to be our perfect fulfillment. Only slowly, through many painful trials and purifications over the years, have we been learning to release each other from these impossible expectations. "After suffering and struggling together," writes Pope Francis, "spouses are able to experience that it was worth it, because they achieved some good, learned something as a couple, or came to appreciate what they have. Few human joys are as deep and thrilling as those experienced by two people who love one another and have achieved something as the result of a great, shared effort" (*The Joy of Love*, 130).

That's why our conversation at the restaurant was cause for rejoicing. The sufferings we had been through together were teaching us something critical: how to stop expecting the other to be God for us, and how to take our yearning for perfect fulfillment to the one who alone can satisfy it. Pope Francis offers some very helpful insights into this dynamic in the following passage from *The Joy of Love*:

> There comes a point where a couple's love attains the height of its freedom and becomes the basis of a healthy autonomy. This happens when each spouse realizes that the other is not his or her own, but has a much more important master, the one Lord. No one but God can presume to take over the deepest and most personal core of the loved one; he alone can be the ultimate center of their life. At the same time, the principle of spiritual realism requires that one spouse not presume that the other can completely satisfy his or her needs. The spiritual journey of each . . . needs to help them through a certain "disillusionment" with regard to the other, to stop expecting from that person something which is proper to the love of God alone. This demands an interior divestment. The space which each of the spouses makes exclusively for their personal relationship with God not only helps heal the hurts of life in common, but also enables the spouses to find in the love of God the deepest source of meaning in their own lives. (320)

Lord, save me from my idols, from all my substitutes for you. Teach me to love you above all things so that I can love all things properly in you.

In what ways do I demand perfection from human love? How does this affect me when the imperfections of others inevitably surface?

We all worship something, whatever we think will satisfy our deepest desires. Where do I seek fulfillment for my deepest desires? In other words, what do I worship?

What is one "heart's desire" that I am trusting God to fulfill? How do I show him that I trust him to do this?

TWELVE

Love Believes All Things

Here "belief" is not to be taken in its strict theological meaning, but more in the sense of what we mean by "trust." This goes beyond simply presuming that the other is not lying or cheating. Such basic trust recognizes God's light shining beyond the darkness, like an ember glowing beneath the ash. (114)

A woman once shared with me the painful story of how her husband had failed to love her in a thousand ways. When she mentioned that the brokenness of his humanity became evident to her during their engagement and she knew ahead of time that it was going to be a rocky road, I asked her why on earth she had still gone through with it. She said she also saw real goodness in him and she firmly believed that eventually that goodness would triumph and it would all be worth it. I could barely speak. . . . The woman telling me all this was my wife.

Love believes all things, trusting in the "ember glowing beneath the ash." Sometimes I'm too focused on the ash to recognize the ember, or even believe it's there. Lord, teach me to see; teach me to believe; teach me to love!

———————————

What contrary attitudes must I expose in my heart in order to believe all things in the sense that Pope Francis outlines in the preceding quote?

Think of someone close to you.
Where is the "ember beneath the ash" in that person?
How can you affirm the light within him or her?

Love trusts, it sets free, it does not try to control, possess and dominate everything. This freedom, which fosters independence, an openness to the world around us and to new experiences, can only enrich and expand relationships. The spouses then share with one another the joy of all they have received and learned outside the family circle. (115)

I remember Wendy's mother having a pretty direct conversation with the two of us during our engagement. With a marked displeasure aimed primarily at me, she was concerned that we were spending too much time together and that Wendy was cutting herself off from her friends and her family in unhealthy ways. I ignored the challenge by convincing myself that Wendy's mom just didn't understand young love. Years later I would realize she was on to something, but I was too proud (and too afraid) during our engagement to look at it.

The truth is, when we were engaged, I was placing subtle (and sometimes not-so-subtle) pressure on Wendy to spend almost all her free time with me. There were occasions when she needed to pursue her interests, foster other friendships, or spend time with her family, and in my insecurity, I found that threatening at some level. Part of me wanted to be the all-consuming center of her life. Unhealthy relating in past relationships had put the seriously misguided notion in my head that that's what love entails. The fact that Wendy didn't think that (and didn't want it) threw me off. When she wanted time to be with her family or her girlfriends and encouraged me to go have a weekend with the guys, it made me think she didn't love me as much as I loved her.

But who wasn't loving whom here?

Sometime after my mother-in-law died, several years into married life, I had a dream about her. She was young and beautiful and was talking with me about how my insecurities had affected my relationship with Wendy. In the dream, I was all ears, and I apologized for not listening to her all those years previously. She was joyful, laughing, and lovingly poking fun at me, as if to say, "Everything's gonna be all right. Keep growing. God has you in his hands. You can trust that he will bring to completion the work he's begun in you."

> Love trusts and sets free. Sometimes
> I dominate and try to control.
> Lord, teach me to love.

How have my personal insecurities affected the way I relate
with others? In what subtle or not-so-subtle ways do
I try to control how those I love spend their time?

How can I foster the freedom and independence of
the people I love?

**[T]hose who know that they are trusted and appreciated
can be open and hide nothing. Those who know that
their spouse is always suspicious, judgmental and lacking
unconditional love, will tend to keep secrets, conceal their
failings and weaknesses, and pretend to be someone other
than who they are. (115)**

Hiding. It's the first result of original sin: "I was afraid, because I
was naked, so I hid myself" (Genesis 3:10). Volumes could be (and
have been) written about that fear. In short, it's a fear that we're
not lovable in our broken, sinful state as human beings. Faith
in God's unconditional love casts this fear out (see 1 John 4:18),
enabling us to bring all of our brokenness into the light, knowing
we will not be rejected, chided, or condemned, but embraced,
comforted, forgiven. This is the kind of love spouses are meant
to share with one another: the love that allows them to be "naked
without shame" (Genesis 2:25). As we know well, it's at the
deepest spiritual level of our humanity—not merely the physical
level—that we're afraid of our nakedness and thus find ourselves
hiding. True love, however, is not afraid of the other person's

"warts." And those who know they are loved unconditionally are not afraid of revealing their warts.

I've long accepted the *idea* that God loves me unconditionally, but internalizing that truth is another matter, and, oh man, has it been a battle! Remember the story of my witnessing Wendy sing to her great grandmother? We were barely boyfriend and girlfriend at that point, but I proposed to her only a month later. One of the reasons I leaped to marry her was because in experiencing the way she so generously loved people, including me, I somehow intuited that this woman could help save me from the cage of fear in which I was trapped—fear that I was not lovable in my real humanity. That, as I've been sharing, was my paradigm.

Recall, however, that I was simultaneously deeply attracted to and profoundly threatened by Wendy's freedom from my paradigm. My true self (the inner self behind the mask) was attracted because I was longing to emerge from a lifetime of hiding. My false self (the outer mask) was threatened because I would have to remove the armor I had clung to my whole life—and the thought of that scared me to death.

These two selves have battled it out for dominance in my life. For much of our early marriage, the false self held sway. Rather than let Wendy's view that I was lovable in my imperfect humanity change me, I set out in some ways to change her to conform to the lies that molded me. So instead of learning how to bring my imperfections into the light (too scary!), I was teaching Wendy that her imperfections had to be hidden. Rather than my learning that I was loved unconditionally, Wendy was learning that she was loved *if.* . . .

None of this was malicious or even conscious on my part. It's just what happened, what came out of me as a result of my fallen, sinful humanity and the painful experiences that shaped me growing up. This is why it is so important, as Pope Francis says, that we "learn to pray over our past history" (*The Joy of Love*, 107).

Here's one such experience. A few years ago, the following memory came vividly to mind while I was praying. When I was seven years old, a kid in my neighborhood named Phil swiped a pack of cigarettes from his dad and invited me to join him in lighting up and taking some puffs. When Phil's dad found out, I was gripped by the fear that he would call my dad. I remember hopping up on the couch next to my dad to see if he knew. When he put his arm around me and drew me close, I knew he didn't. His affection meant all was well. So I scampered off to play outside, happily thinking I was off the hook. Not ten minutes later, fear grabbed me by the throat when my dad came outside shouting sternly, "*CHRISTOPHER! In the house right now!*"

My father, of course, had every right to discipline me, and everyone must learn that wrongdoing causes a certain rupture in our relationships. But as a boy yearning for his father's affection, the pain of "losing" his affection when I did something wrong contributed to a pattern in me of hiding my faults from others to "maintain" or "win" their love. Opening up this memory in prayer, I sensed the heavenly Father whisper, "You think I won't love you if your faults are on display. You think I withdraw my affection whenever you fail." The whisper insisted, this time in more than a whisper, "No! I want to draw you even closer to my side. That's where you find my mercy. But I can't do that if you're hiding from me."

Mercy. The Latin *misericordia* means "a heart that gives itself to those in misery," or "having a heart for the misery of others." I grew up thinking my misery repulsed God. Only through praying over my past history have I come to learn that my misery actually draws God to me. That changes everything. It means the light is my friend. It means *exposing* my heart, not hiding it, is the key to experiencing the heavenly Father's closeness.

Prayer, true contemplative "being" in God's presence, the *Catechism* tells us, is where we "let our masks fall and turn our hearts back to the Lord who loves us, so as to hand ourselves over to him as an offering to be purified and transformed" (2711). Always with a tender love for us, the Lord accomplishes this inner purification through painful trials that the mystical tradition calls "strippings," "denudings," or "dark nights." In his book *Interior Freedom,* Father Jacques Philippe describes this phenomenon as follows:

> The trials or "purifications" so frequently referred to by the mystics are there to destroy whatever is artificial in our character, so that our true being may emerge.... The [dark] night of the soul could be called a series of impoverishments, sometimes violent ones, that strip believers of all possibility of relying on themselves. These trials are beneficial, because they lead us to locate our identity where it truly belongs . . . [They also deprive] us of any possibility of relying on [ourselves and] the good that we can do. God's mercy is all. . . . Progressively, and in a way that parallels their terrible impoverishment, those who go through such trials while still hoping in the Lord, begin to realize the truth of something that up until then was only a pious expression: God loves us in an absolutely unconditional way, by virtue of himself, his mercy, and his infinite tenderness, by virtue of his Fatherhood towards us.

As Pope Francis affirms, it's only by accepting God's unconditional love that we become capable of showing that same love to others. It's as simple as recognizing, once again, that we can't give what we don't have. Slowly, painfully, through many purifications and trials, the ship is getting turned around in my life and I am learning what for a long time was only a pious expression: God really loves me in an absolutely unconditional way. Adam's fear in me is slowly getting reversed. "I was afraid, because I was naked, so I hid myself" is becoming "I was at peace, because I knew you loved me, so I exposed myself." Experiencing the joy of that nakedness before God is precisely experiencing *the joy of love.*

> **Love is unconditional. Sometimes I put conditions on my love, subtly saying or implying I'll love you *if.* . . . Lord, teach me to love.**
>
> ---
>
> In what ways am I hiding from God, projecting onto him the same kind of rejection and pain I've experienced from others?
>
> Is the notion that God loves me unconditionally just a pious idea or a lived experience in my life? What are some of the practical ways he makes his love real to me?

THIRTEEN

Love Hopes All Things

[T]his phrase speaks of the hope of one who knows that others can change, mature and radiate unexpected beauty and untold potential. This does not mean that everything will change in this life. It does involve realizing that, though things may not always turn out as we wish, God may well make crooked lines straight and draw some good from the evil we endure in this world. (116)

If I'm living the truth of love, that love buoys me in times of darkness and hardship, in times in which I'm forced to endure various sufferings and evils, even great sufferings and great evils. That buoy is love hoping all things.

Hoping all things is not wishful thinking that life will get better on its own or the naive optimism that things will eventually go my way if I just think positively. Those who hope all things don't turn a blind eye to their own or others' misfortune. Instead, with full reckoning of the evils and sufferings of this world, hope is unwaveringly confident that God can and will transform all those evils and sufferings into glory. In fact, while we are still awaiting its complete realization in our lives, hope knows well that God already *has* transformed them in the death and resurrection of his Son.

The *Catechism* observes that faith in God "can be put to the test by the experience of evil and suffering. God can sometimes seem to be absent and incapable of stopping evil. But in the most mysterious way God the Father has revealed his almighty power in the voluntary humiliation and resurrection of his Son, by which he conquered evil" (272). Christ's glorified wounds are the certainty that good can come from evil, beauty from ugliness, radiance from darkness. *That* is our hope. Love hopes all things because it is inextricably plugged into the current of Christ's Passover from sorrow to joy, from agony to ecstasy, from mourning to laughing, from humiliation to exaltation, from rupture to communion, from death to new life. The *Catechism* goes on to say, quoting St. Augustine, that because God "is supremely good, [he] would never allow any evil whatsoever to exist in his works if he were not so all-powerful and good as to cause good to emerge from evil itself" (311).

Flowers from wounds—that's the image that once came to me as a symbol of what Wendy and I were experiencing in living out our own passion narrative, our own experience of dying and rising with Christ. I've spoken at some length in these reflections of how I've wounded my wife, but, of course, it's been a two-way street; we've wounded each other. Those wounds, opened up to the Master Gardener, become openings in the soil for his fertile seeds to enter and take root—flowers from wounds.

It can be tempting, especially when old wounds and unhealthy patterns of relating resurface, to fall into despair: "Am I *ever* going to learn?" "Is she *ever* going to change?" But love hopes all things. Nothing enlivens that hope more than stopping and remembering to smell the flowers that have come from wounds.

> Love hopes all things. Sometimes I get bogged down and discouraged. Lord, teach me to love.

In what ways has God made crooked lines straight in my life? How has he brought good out of an evil I've endured?

Are there wounds in my life that I've buried rather than opened up to Christ? Do I believe the Master Gardener can bring flowers from my wounds?

Write a prayer in your own words asking for the grace to hope all things, whatever crises you may face or evils you may be asked to endure.

[H]ope comes most fully into its own [when] it embraces the certainty of life after death. Each person, with all his or her failings, is called to the fullness of life in heaven. There, fully transformed by Christ's resurrection, every weakness, darkness and infirmity will pass away. There the person's true being will shine forth in all its goodness and beauty. This realization helps us, amid the aggravations of this present life, to see each person from a supernatural

perspective, in the light of hope, and await the fullness that he or she will receive in the heavenly kingdom, even if it is not yet visible. (117)

As C. S. Lewis wrote in his marvelous book *The Weight of Glory*:

> It is a serious thing to live in a society of possible gods and goddesses, to remember that the dullest most uninteresting person you can talk to may one day be a creature which, if you saw it now, you would be strongly tempted to worship. . . .

Acknowledging the option of refusing heaven, Lewis also notes the possibility for each of us to become "a horror and a corruption such as you now meet, if at all, only in a nightmare. All day long we are, in some degree helping each other to one or the other of these destinations," he concludes. And this means that there "are no ordinary people. You have never talked to a mere mortal. . . . [I]t is immortals whom we joke with, work with, marry, snub, and exploit. . . ."

In light of these astounding truths, whenever I'm tempted to look at others wrongly (with annoyance, superiority, lust, dismissal, or what have you), I'm trying to cultivate the habit of saying to myself, "I want to see your eternal glory." Or "Lord, help me to see this person in light of the glory you want to give him (or her)." It puts everything in perspective for me and snaps me out of my temptation. It also opens my heart to hope.

"The virtue of hope responds to the aspiration to happiness which God has placed in the heart of every man," says the

Catechism. It opens up our hearts in expectation of eternal life (see 1818). But what does that even mean? Eternal life "is not an unending succession of days on the calendar," observed Pope Benedict XVI, "but something more like the supreme moment of satisfaction in which totality embraces us and we embrace totality." It is "like plunging into the ocean of infinite love . . . a plunging ever anew into the vastness of being, in which we are simply overwhelmed with joy. . . . We must think along these lines if we want . . . to understand what it is that our faith leads us to expect" (*Spe Salvi*, 12).

Most of us have seriously impoverished, disincarnate impressions of heaven: an eternal boredom of harps and halos, or an eternal prayer meeting in the sky, in which all we do is bow before God as he reclines on his throne. What's to hope for in that? While eye has not seen and ear has not heard what God has ready for those who love him, this we know: All of creation (including our bodies!) will be restored and glorified; all injustices will be addressed; all wrongs will be righted; all sorrow and suffering eliminated; and the ache, the constant craving we've known here on earth, will be filled with all the fullness of divine love, affording an ecstasy and a bliss beyond what we can dream or imagine.

An integral part of this heavenly expectation is *seeing* and *participating in* other people's glorified humanity. It's called the communion of saints, and it will provide a transparent and transcendent joy in our relationships with one and all. In all our dealings with others in the here and now, we must cultivate the hope of one day knowing and rejoicing in their fully redeemed and unrepeatable beauty and goodness while resisting all the forces that militate against it.

For example, I've been wrestling a lot lately with the reality of aging. My wife and I are getting older. Our heads are graying, our muscles are fatiguing, and our skin is wrinkling. And it's only going to continue in that direction, of course; there's no turning back the clock. The loss of the physical beauty and vitality of youth is one of those "aggravations of this present life." And I'm feeling it. Recently at Mass I noticed a young, attractive woman sitting next to her grandmother, who was bent over with age and infirmity. There it was—the life span before my eyes. That elderly woman was once young and attractive and full of life, like her granddaughter. And that granddaughter will one day be bent over with age and infirmity, like her grandmother. In the midst of my ponderings, I found this question descend upon me: Who is closer to glory?

It dawned on me: If I'm looking nostalgically *backward* to the fleeting and fading vitality of youth to satisfy my desire for life, I'm looking the wrong way. And my tendency to look in that direction is itself a testimony—despite any confession to the contrary—that I don't *really* believe in the Resurrection, at least not in a way that shapes my daily thoughts and attitudes. If the death and resurrection of Christ is real and I've been baptized into it, then the satisfaction of my heart-aching desire for lasting life, love, and beauty is found not by looking backward, but by looking *forward*, pressing on to what lies ahead, because "hope does not disappoint" (Romans 5:5). Without this hope, I find my heart clinging to the idol of youth, and to the degree that I do, every gray hair, every age spot, every wrinkle my wife and I get becomes a threat. With this hope of future glory, however, I can accept my wife's and my aging with peace and serenity.

It's not a pleasant thought, but every one of us is on an unstoppable conveyor belt headed for the drop-off called death.

When love fails to hope in the Resurrection, men divorce their wives after thirty years and shack up with much younger women. When love fails to hope in the Resurrection, we turn to makeup and cosmetic surgery to maintain the illusion of youthfulness. "In the course of every marriage physical appearances change," reflects Pope Francis. But if love hopes all things, "love and attraction [don't] fade. We love the other person for who they are, not simply for [the appearance of] their body. Although the body ages, it still expresses that personal identity that first won our heart. Even if others can no longer see the beauty of that identity, a spouse continues to see it with the eyes of love and so his or her affection does not diminish" (*The Joy of Love*, 164).

Lord, I fear death. May your perfect love cast out my fear. Teach me to hope all things.

When I face the reality and fear of aging and dying, where do I place my hope (not where do I think I'm supposed to place it, but where do I actually place it)? Am I hoping in science? Am I hoping in medicine or nutrition? Am I hoping in makeup or cosmetic surgery?

The last line of the Apostles' Creed proclaims, "I believe in the resurrection of the body." How do I view the afterlife? Have I superspiritualized it, conceiving of the body as a shell or even a prison from which I hope to escape at death? Where do these impressions come from?

What questions, concerns, fears, and hopes regarding
my death and the deaths of those I love do I have?
Where do I turn to find answers?

FOURTEEN

Love Endures All Things

This means that love bears every trial with a positive attitude. It stands firm in hostile surroundings. This "endurance" involves not only the ability to tolerate certain aggravations, but something greater: a constant readiness to confront any challenge. It is a love that *never gives up*, even in the darkest hour. It shows a certain dogged heroism, a power to resist every negative current, an irrepressible commitment to goodness. (118)

We call ourselves followers of Christ, but where did he go if not straight into the darkest hour, bearing every trial with an "irrepressible commitment to goodness"? The love of man and woman, and the entire reality of marriage and family life that flows from it, bears the sacramental sign of Christ's love for the Church. It would seem with regard to that sacramental sign, we are fast approaching the darkest hour. As this book draws to a close, I would like to reflect on what is happening in our world today with regard to marriage and the family and on how to bear the trial with a positive attitude and an irrepressible commitment to goodness.

We live in a post–sexual revolution world, in which marriages are crumbling and the majority of children are growing up without models of committed love; in which idealized and hyper-eroticized images of the human body have become our cultural wallpaper and people are valued only if they are accordingly stimulating; in which the gross distortions of hard-core pornography have become our main reference point for understanding sexual behavior, and sexual addiction masquerades under the banner of liberation; in which the blessing of fertility is considered a curse to be eliminated and the innocent human life that springs from sexual union a threat to be exterminated; in which governments institutionalize gender confusion and insist that sexual difference has no real meaning or consequence; in which society glorifies those who mutilate their bodies so they can "become" the other sex and vilifies those who raise warning flags; and in which our Christian parents, teachers, pastors, and confessors are largely unable to respond to these challenges in any compelling way for lack of proper formation themselves. In light of all this, we are, indeed, facing the eclipse of the deepest, most fundamental truths of our humanity.

"Marriage is the icon of God's love for us," affirms Pope Francis (*The Joy of Love*, 121). As such, it has been under attack since the beginning. In fact, as St. John Paul II taught us in Theology of the Body, "Sin and death have entered into man's history *in some way through the very heart of that unity that had from the 'beginning' been formed by man and woman*, created and called to become 'one flesh' (Gen 2:24)." But if the enemy entered the sanctuary of married life from the beginning to sow seeds of death and destruction, let us never forget where Christ performed his first miracle: at a wedding that foreshadowed his "hour"—that darkest hour of his crucifixion. This is how redemption comes; unfathomable as it is to human wisdom, the death and resurrection of the Bridegroom is God's method of victory. And marriage "is a reflection of the unbroken covenant between Christ and humanity that culminated in his self-sacrifice on the Cross" (*The Joy of Love,* 120).

We must ponder this; we must let it sink in if we are to understand properly what is happening in our world today: Marriage, it would seem, is going the way of its exemplar. It's being put on trial, condemned, mocked, rejected, spat upon, scourged, and crucified. But give it three days and watch what happens: "On the third day there was a marriage at Cana in Galilee" (John 2:1). Jesus and Mary are always about the business of restoring God's wine to man and woman's relationship, but wine, of course, comes only through the crushing of the grapes and the fermenting of the juice. It comes only through the winepress of the cross, through the pierced side of the Bridegroom and the yes of the woman at the foot of the cross. Setting our gaze here, remaining here at what St. Augustine called "the marriage bed of the Cross," is what will properly orient us amid all the craziness now unfolding.

Our world today talks often enough about sexual orientation, but the most fundamental orientation of sexuality is to point us to Christ and the redemption he won for us through his death and resurrection. Recall the eclipse of the sun that took place on Good Friday (see Luke 23:45). The truth of marriage is experiencing a similar eclipse. But here's our sure hope: *Sunday is not far off.* When "the third day" dawns, God's plan for marriage will be resurrected and the truth of our creation as male and female will shine like the sun! The world will see the light and be reoriented.

That's what the sun does—it *orients* us. That's why the bride (the Church) traditionally prays her liturgy toward the East (the Orient), because the rising of the sun, as the psalmist says, is the symbol of the coming of the Bridegroom (see Psalm 19:5). And when the Bridegroom comes, nothing will be hidden from its burning heat (see Psalm 19:6). As the Church prays in her liturgy, "The glory of the Lord will fill the whole earth, and all flesh will see the salvation of God!"

This is God's promise. We can count on it. It's literally written in the stars. It's also written in our bodies—in every*body*. This is why safeguarding the truth about marriage is not important just for married people. It's critical for every member of the human race so that we can be properly oriented toward our eternal destiny, the marriage of Christ and the Church: "The Spirit and the bride say, 'Come.' . . . 'Surely I am coming soon,'" responds the Bridegroom (Revelation 22:17, 20).

The sure hope of the eternal Bridegroom's coming is what enables us to endure all that is happening in our world right now. As surely as night turns to day, the glory of God revealed through the theology of our bodies as male and female will appear on the horizon and light up the earth. Now, it is true, we must suffer the eclipse. And I'm guessing things will get darker before they get brighter. Yet, as St. Paul reminds us, we should consider the sufferings we must now endure as nothing compared to the glory to be revealed in us (see Romans 8:18). Be not afraid! "Weeping may tarry for the night; but joy comes with the morning" (Psalm 30:5)! Indeed, "the wine press is full; the vats overflow . . . the day of the Lord is near in the valley of decision" (Joel 3:13–14).

Love bears every trial with a positive attitude.
I don't. Lord, teach me to love.

In one way or another, everyone has suffered the fallout of
the sexual revolution. Of those things listed in the litany in the
beginning of this section, which struck me the most?
Which of these have my loved ones and I suffered
from in a direct way?

St. John Paul II boldly held out to the whole world the real
promise and power of the healing of our sexual and relational
wounds in his magnificent Theology of the Body.

*Based on your response to the preceding question,
compose a prayer in your own words asking for the grace
of healing and redemption from whatever you
and your loved ones have suffered most.*

[Quoting Martin Luther King] "Another way that you
love your enemy is this: when the opportunity presents
itself for you to defeat your enemy, that is the time when
you must not do it. . . . Hate for hate only intensifies the
existence of hate and evil in the universe. If I hit you and
you hit me and I hit you back and you hit me back and so
on, you see, that . . . never ends. . . . The strong person is
the person who can cut off the chain of hate, the chain of

evil . . . and inject within the very structure of the universe that strong and powerful element of love." (118)

Think of how David treated Saul. Saul was hunting David down to take his life, and when Saul went into a cave to relieve himself—the cave in which David and his men just so happened to be hiding—David had the opportunity to slay him, but instead he only quietly cut off a piece of his garment. Later, holding up that piece of garment for Saul to see, David said, "You see for yourself today that the Lord just now delivered you into my hand in the cave. I was told to kill you, but I took pity on you instead" (1 Samuel 24:11, NAB). Or think of how Jean Valjean treated Javert in *Les Misérables*. After years of being pursued by Javert and constantly being on the run, the opportunity presented itself for Valjean to end Javert's life. In the musical version of the story, an utterly bewildered Javert sings, "All it would take was a flick of his knife / Vengeance was his and he gave me back my life."

How do we love those who clearly do not love us? Pope Francis quotes Martin Luther King's keen insight: "The person who hates you most has some good in him. . . . And when you come to the point that you look in the face of every man and see deep down within him . . . 'the image of God,' you begin to love him in spite of [everything]. No matter what he does, you see God's image there" (118).

Here's a remarkable story of such love. A priest student of mine pulled me aside after class one day. I had just been teaching in that session about the miracle that can happen when we open the pain people cause us to the Holy Spirit—hurt becomes compassion, and compassion becomes love and intercession. I listened attentively as he told me about the pastoral work he did as a priest. He had requested of his bishop and was granted the assignment of serving those whom many consider the most wretched and undeserving of all: priests guilty of sexually abusing children. He said that he felt a great burden of love for these priests and knew he was meant to dedicate his own priesthood to ministering God's merciful, healing graces to them. Then he revealed in a reserved way, "I was sexually abused by a priest when I was a boy." I could barely speak.

Love endures all things for the sake of transforming all that the world endures into love. This is the miracle of the cross. Jesus, help me to enter into this miracle of love.

What sins in my own life or the lives of others do I think are perhaps beyond the reach of God's mercy?

Have I withheld forgiveness from anyone who has wounded me? How can I surrender those who have hurt me to God's mercy and justice?

How can I see the image of God in someone who has hurt me deeply?

I am sometimes amazed to see men or women who have had to separate from their spouse for their own protection, yet, because of their enduring conjugal love, still try to

help them, even by enlisting others, in their moments of illness, suffering or trial. Here too we see a love that never gives up. (119)

I come from a big family. My mother was the oldest of eleven (not unusual for an Irish Catholic family in the mid-twentieth century), so family gatherings were quite an affair. My mother's uncle George stood out in the family as the only unmarried person of that generation. Bachelor though he was, he did have a "lady friend" who came with him to family gatherings. I remember as a boy some of the chatter about his situation, as people wondered aloud why Uncle George and his lady friend didn't tie the knot. Finally, several years into their relationship, they did.

As it turns out, Uncle George's lady friend had been married as a young woman but was subsequently abandoned by her husband. Decades later, after reading in the newspaper that the man she had married all those years earlier had died, she said to George, "Now I can marry you."

That story left a big impression on me as a young person. Fidelity to her wedding vows meant something to her. Even though her first husband had given up on her, she had never given up on him. That is a love that endures all things. And isn't that how we wish to be loved? We *are* loved that way by Love itself; by Love himself: "If we are faithless, he remains faithful" (2 Timothy 2:13).

As Pope Francis proclaimed in his Lenten message of 2016, "As the Son of God, [Christ] is the Bridegroom who does everything to win over the love of his bride, to whom he is bound by an unconditional love which becomes visible in the eternal wedding feast. This is the very heart of the apostolic kerygma, in which divine mercy holds a central and fundamental place." *Apostolic kerygma* means the Church's initial and essential proclamation of the gospel message. And here it is: God wants to marry us. That's the whole Bible in five words. And we want to marry God. It's the deepest yearning of the human heart—to be immersed in infinite love. Jesus, you *are* the marriage of God and man. May we come to desire what we truly desire and settle for nothing less than the full truth of LOVE:

> Love is patient and kind;
> love is not jealous or boastful;
> it is not arrogant or rude.
> Love does not insist on its own way,
> it is not irritable or resentful;
> it does not rejoice at wrong,
> but rejoices in the right.
> Love bears all things,
> believes all things,
> hopes all things,
> endures all things.
> Love never fails.

Lord, teach me to love!

What are the three most important things I have gained
or learned from reading this book?

What are three resolutions I want to make in order to live
the joy of love more fully in my life?

*Write a prayer in your own words asking for the grace to
be faithful to those resolutions.*

CONCLUSION

In his Theology of the Body, St. John Paul II spoke of three "infallible and indispensable" means for living an authentic marital spirituality (these apply just as well, of course, to any Christian life):

A deepening life of prayer
Regular confession of our sins
Frequent reception of the Eucharist

At first, this might just sound like "standard Catholic stuff" that you've heard before. Sure enough, it is. But John Paul II's "spousal theology" gives us a fresh, *mystical* perspective that you probably didn't hear about growing up in the Church. I'd like to conclude this book by taking a brief look at how his "spousal lenses" illuminate this path of authentic marital spirituality.

A Deepening Life of Prayer. The fathers of the Church tell us that prayer is nothing other than becoming a longing for God. If we have the courage to follow it the whole way through, this longing, says St. John Paul II, will take us through "painful purifications (the 'dark night'). But it leads, in various possible ways, to the ineffable joy experienced by the mystics as 'nuptial union'" . . . with the Lord (*Novo Millennio Ineunte*, 33). Engaging in prayer, therefore, in a nutshell, means getting in touch with our deepest, most real, most honest desires for love and union and opening them up to the one who alone can satisfy them.

Regular Confession of Our Sins. Whenever we commit serious sin, we should be going to confession. That may mean quite frequently for lots of us. But this does not mean we should not also be going regularly if we haven't done anything "big, bad, and horrible." As the *Catechism* says, "Without being strictly necessary, confession of everyday faults (venial sins) is nevertheless strongly recommended by the Church. Indeed the regular confession of our venial sins helps us form our conscience, fight against evil tendencies, let ourselves be healed by Christ and progress in the life of the Spirit" (1458). If we're taking our journey seriously, we should be going to confession at least once a month. Prayerful reception of this sacrament is where we "let our masks fall and turn our hearts back to the Lord who loves us, so as to hand ourselves over to him as an offering to be purified and transformed" (2711). In other words, confession is where we "get naked" before God and allow Christ to wash his bride (see Ephesians 5:27) so as to prepare her for "nuptial union"—the Eucharist.

Frequent Reception of the Eucharist. The Eucharist, wrote St. John Paul II, is "the sacrament of the Bridegroom and of the Bride." Christ instituted the Eucharist, he continued, "to express the relationship between man and woman, between what is 'feminine' and what is 'masculine'" (*Mulieris Dignitatem*, 26). Such a wealth of truth is contained in these statements! In the Eucharist, Christ the Bridegroom gives up his body for his bride and we, the bride, receive his body into ours. In short, if prayer is getting in touch with our desire for nuptial union and confession is getting naked before God, the Eucharist is the consummation of the marriage.

At the close of this book, I urge you to recommit yourself to these three infallible and indispensable means of becoming the men and women we are created to be. They're infallible because when they are properly understood and lived, they can't possibly steer us wrong, and they're indispensable because we simply can't live the Christian life to the fullest without them.

I also urge you to take up a study of St. John Paul II's Theology of the Body. Here are a few ways you can do that:

If you have the aptitude, read the actual text: *Man and Woman He Created Them: A Theology of the Body* (Pauline, 2006).

If you, like most people, need help understanding the dense, scholarly teaching of St. John Paul II, several authors have written books and study guides to help you receive the riches he gave us. Google "theology of the body resources" to find them.

If you enjoy my approach, visit my ministry's website, corproject.com, and click on "shop" for a full listing of books, CDs, DVDs, study programs, and more. I'd suggest starting with *Theology of the Body for Beginners* or *Fill These Hearts: God, Sex, and the Universal Longing*.

If you would like ongoing formation in the Theology of the Body, consider joining a worldwide community of men and women who are learning, living, and sharing this teaching as members of the Cor Project. Visit cormembership.com to learn more.

Consider taking a five-day immersion course in this liberating vision of life and love through the Theology of the Body Institute. Learn more at tobinstitute.org.

ACKNOWLEDGMENTS

My gratitude goes out to the following people who helped bring this book to completion: Wendy West, Jason Clark, Bill Howard, Rose Sweet, Fr. Peter O'Donnell, Matthew Kelly, and all the staff at Beacon.

ABOUT THE AUTHOR

Christopher West is a proud husband and father of five. He is also the world's most recognized teacher and promoter of St. John Paul II's Theology of the Body. As founder and president of the Cor Project, he leads a global outreach and membership organization devoted to helping others learn, live, and share this liberating teaching. He is also a cofounder of the Theology of the Body Institute; the intensive courses he teaches there attract students from around the world. His extensive lecturing and numerous best-selling books, articles, and video programs have sparked an international groundswell of interest in the Theology of the Body, and his work has been featured in the *New York Times*; on ABC News, Fox News, and MSNBC; and in countless Catholic and Protestant media outlets.

Blessed

THE DYNAMIC CATHOLIC FIRST COMMUNION & FIRST RECONCILIATION EXPERIENCE

There's never been anything like this for children:
World-class animation. Workbooks with 250 hand-painted
works of art. Catechist-friendly leader guides, and incredible
content. Blessed isn't just different, it's groundbreaking.

Request your **FREE** First Communion Program Pack &
First Reconciliation Program Pack
at *DynamicCatholic.com/BlessedPack.*

EACH PROGRAM PACK INCLUDES:

- 1 DVD SET (42 ANIMATED SHORT FILMS)
- 1 STUDENT WORKBOOK
- 1 LEADER GUIDE
- 1 CHILDREN'S PRAYER PROCESS CARD

Just pay shipping.

Dynamic Catholic
Be Bold. Be Catholic.®

THE
DYNAMIC CATHOLIC
INSTITUTE

[MISSION]

To re-energize the Catholic Church in America by developing world-class resources that inspire people to rediscover the genius of Catholicism.

[VISION]

To be the innovative leader in the New Evangelization helping Catholics and their parishes become the-best-version-of-themselves.

Join us in re-energizing the Catholic Church.
Become a Dynamic Catholic Ambassador today!

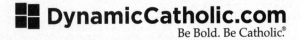

DynamicCatholic.com
Be Bold. Be Catholic.®